THE MANAGEMENT TEAM

The Management Team

EDITED BY
EDWARD C. BURSK
EDITOR OF THE *Harvard Business Review* AND
PROFESSOR OF BUSINESS ADMINISTRATION
HARVARD GRADUATE SCHOOL OF BUSINESS ADMINISTRATION

CAMBRIDGE, MASSACHUSETTS
HARVARD UNIVERSITY PRESS
1954

First printing December 1954

Distributed in Great Britain by
GEOFFREY CUMBERLEGE
OXFORD UNIVERSITY PRESS
LONDON

Library of Congress Catalog Card Number 55-5980
Printed in the United States of America

PREFACE

This book, the seventh in an annual series published by the Harvard University Press, is based on the proceedings of the Twenty-Fourth National Business Conference, sponsored by the Harvard Business School Association, June 12, 1954, which was attended by some 1,300 businessmen — alumni and friends of the School — from all over the country and abroad.

The general theme of the Conference was "Releasing the Full Potential of the Management Team." The morning session, consisting of four speeches that develop the major company policies needed for this purpose, is covered in Part I. The afternoon session, consisting of seven panels that deal with specific areas of management, is covered in Part II.

The afternoon panels were conducted purposely on a very informal basis, in an attempt to let the subject develop as the group desired. Short talks by the panel members, aimed primarily at providing factual material from their own experience and establishing their individual positions within the general subject area, were followed by a question and answer period. As happened at previous Conferences, the discussion which ensued was dynamic and spontaneous; and all together it took up the major portion of the afternoon. For the most part, this material has been reorganized into orderly form and fitted into the chapter-sections representing the observations of the various panel members.

Needless to say, the views expressed in any chapter or chapter-section are the responsibility of the individual author, and as such are not necessarily representative of other authors or the Harvard Business School Association.

I want to thank Miss Louise B. Morse, Miss Corinne S. Benson, and Miss Virginia B. Fales for their very able editorial assistance.

Edward C. Bursk

CONTENTS

PART I

PART II

PART I

INTRODUCTION OF THE THEME: RELEASING THE FULL POTENTIAL OF THE MANAGEMENT TEAM

By Donald K. David *

I am happy to welcome readers to this book, which is based on the Twenty-Fourth National Business Conference at the Harvard Business School.

This is the most recent in the series of books based on similar conferences over the past six years — or, as I prefer to think of it, the series of meetings where businessmen, whether through attendance at the conference or through reading of the book, participate in exploring significant aspects of the administrative process.

I am proud of the way in which these conferences, and their published counterparts, provide each year a more noteworthy symbol of progress in the achievement of professional skills and professional standards for business management, and a greater opportunity for bringing together the two great communities of business and education, so interdependent for strength and power.

The subject to be explored here is of critical importance to all businessmen, no matter what industry, company, or specialty they represent. *Releasing the full potential of the management team* is a central task of the responsible executive and one of his principal obligations regardless of his rank or assignment.

Anyone who has attended the previous conferences or read the books based on them knows that they all have been devoted to examination of the tasks of the administrator and the abilities and points of view which lead to *effectiveness in administration.* But the idea of "effectiveness" includes not only success in competition

* Mr. David has been Dean of the Harvard University Graduate School of Business Administration since 1942. He was previously President of American Maize-Products Company, and before that President of Royal Baking Powder.

and profitable operation but also the responsible role of the businessman in community and world affairs, as a citizen and as a leader obligated to serve the larger community outside his own company. And the idea of "administration" grows with the imagination and aspiration which is applied to its study in the many concrete experiences that the Harvard Business School shares with business, all helping to clarify and make tangible and practical the worthiest connotations of business leadership and the professional character of administration.

Our concept of the administrative process, then, carries us far beyond the conventional picture of administration as organized exploitation of individual activity. Similarly, the concepts of delegation and control take on a new perspective as we take a fresh look at them. Delegation and control are the principal functions for the development of the greatest potential effectiveness of a management team. And free communication must be achieved before extensive delegation and effective control become possible. Knowing how to delegate, how to exercise control, and how to achieve free communication are essential skills of the executive.

Without delegation so extensive that it involves real risk — the placing of bets on people's ability — individuals in an organization cannot develop the competence which makes delegation possible. We begin to believe that delegation better serves its purpose when we take chances on subordinates than when we hesitate for fear they will fall short. Responsibility can probably be learned only when it is fully given. It may be essential to the individual development without which a management team cannot be effective that men work at tasks which are a little beyond their capacity.

At the same time, delegation without control is irresponsible. Just as delegation involves taking risks on the capacity of others, the exercise of control includes the risk that delegation be inhibited and freedom of action be restricted. Control systems can stifle the spirit which the most dynamic kind of delegation requires. Striking the balance in concrete situations between uncontrolled activity and excessive checking up is a recurring task of the administrator.

The intricate paradoxes involved in the process of delegation and control will occupy much of this book. Let me call particular attention to one proposition in which I wholeheartedly believe: that the strength of any organization or any part of an organization increases with the ability of people at all levels to accept responsibility. The administrator delegates responsibility to the people below him. By the exercise of control over the activities delegated, he is informed of the quality of the work delegated. He then gives attention to qualifying men to discharge better the responsibility delegated to them. Rather than hold the responsibilities assigned to any person or any group at a static level, he tries to arrange that these responsibilities should continually exceed the capacities of individuals by a sufficient margin to challenge them to reach *forward* for strength and *upward* in the quality of their contribution to the company.

Realizing the potentialities of the organizations in which we work means not only success and strength to our companies but the attainment as well of our full powers as individuals. Essential to satisfying participation in organized affairs is our realization that we are continually moving forward in our grasp of what we are doing and what needs to be done.

In this direction lie the rewards of professional management which, I have often said, can exceed the satisfactions of financial returns. At any rate, it is this interest in moving forward that occasions the exploring we are about to engage in—you who read along with those who write. I hope that, as we think together, you will find the ideas which are generated to be rewarding, and that you will experience some forward impetus to your own professional endeavors.

THE ART OF DELEGATION

*By Lucius D. Clay**

My assignment is to discuss the art of delegation. I am very glad indeed that delegation is classified as an art rather than a science. Art has been defined as human contrivance or ingenuity, as in adapting natural things to man's use; or as the general principles of any branch of learning or of any craft, as the art of war. However, art is also defined as cunning and artifice; and perhaps, as applied to the delegation of authority and responsibility, there may come times when even a little cunning and some artifice will be needed to stimulate and develop the will to accept responsibility and the courage to exercise authority.

In any event, an organization can never be really depicted either in beautifully planned charts or precise definitions of duties, because basically it must be composed of human beings. Its success depends on so relating these human beings to one another as to draw from them collectively their best efforts. Of course we must have organizational charts if only to know what we seek, although they may become meaningless unless the individuals who fill the spaces have the capacities to absorb the responsibilities. Even then those individuals with above average capacities will continually absorb the work and responsibilities of their weaker associates. As a result, the incompetence or unwillingness of an individual to accept responsibility may go undiscovered for months or years.

I am not given to definitions, and thus I find it difficult to express what is meant by the broad term "delegation." Presumably, we are

* General Clay, who gave the address on which this chapter is based, has been Chairman of the Board of Directors of Continental Can Company since 1950. Prior to that time he served in the United States Army, holding such positions as Director of Materiel for the Army, Deputy Director for War Mobilization and Reconversion, and Commander in Chief of the U. S. Forces in Europe and Military Governor of Germany (in which capacity he directed the famous Berlin Airlift in 1949).

dividing the responsibilities which accrue in the management of a business into compartments headed by individuals who are given the required authority to deal with the responsibilities which are theirs and to represent these responsibilities in their associations within the management group.

A decentralized management is one in which there has been a broad delegation of authority and responsibility. For example, each product division in our company is headed by a general manager who is held responsible for profits and, therefore, under general company policies must make the decisions which influence profits.

Often it is said that if delegation of authority is to be successful, then the responsibility and the degree of authority to be delegated must be spelled out in clear, unmistakable terms, so that not only the individual to whom responsibility is delegated will know the limits of his authority, but also that others in the organization will have a clear understanding. Although in theory I subscribe to this tenet, I would never be satisfied with the individual who is not continually seeking to add to his responsibilities, to increase his authority, and who in case of doubt never hesitates to make decisions which are not being made by others perhaps more directly responsible. It is in the give-and-take of such exercise of authority that the arguments, the differences of opinion, and finally the reconciliations of views develop to make a team out of a group of individuals, and it is this give-and-take that assures top management of views matured in a conflict of ideas rather than from a crystal ball.

Tradition has it that the tendency of man to organize, including the delegation of authority, was an outgrowth of his desire for security. The earliest military commanders, realizing their inability to be at all places on the battlefield at the same time, appointed deputy commanders and assigned to them specific missions to guide their conduct in battle. Perhaps, however, the delegation of authority started even earlier as tribal groupings became too large for one man to rule, thus paving the way for a more formal application of organizational principles to armies and to religious groups.

However, the adoption of the organizational structure long associated with government and with religious groups, which divides responsibility, delegates authority, and provides expert staff assistance to assure co-ordination, came in comparatively modern times to the industrial world. The growth of large industrial complexes beyond the ability of a single man, or even a few men, to administer has come about as part of the age in which we now live.

Perhaps the first consideration in the delegation of responsibility is the selection of those to whom authority is to be granted. Seldom can this be done anew in any organization; rather it is the process of training those already within the organization or of finding new men to replace those who cannot be trained and to meet future requirements.

Thus, there is ever the problem of improving the performances of those who exercise executive responsibility. To this end, they are provided with adequate staff assistance; accounting returns to furnish up-to-date information on production, sales, and costs; labor experts concerned with the improvement of worker productivity, the operation of training programs, and the bettering of labor relations; commercial research studies on the acceptability of products as compared with competitive offerings. Statistical data beyond the capacity of the individual to absorb are analyzed, summarized, and made available in convenient form to the business executive. Probably he has also been assigned goals or quotas to achieve, and a budget under which he must live as he struggles to accomplish his objectives.

All of this should create the climate for the growth of the ideal executive. However, no amount of information or of staff assistance can establish the human relationships which are the real problems of the executive. Until he has found a way to develop understanding and confidence between and among his associates and his assistants, he has not demonstrated the leadership qualities which will carry him into positions of increasing responsibility.

Hence, management is faced with its most difficult problem: How is it to find the potential executive who is willing to accept responsibility and prepared to make the hard decisions which result? There is always the easy path: saying to yourself that once a responsibility is assigned to a specific executive, it no longer concerns you except to replace the man who fails in execution. Such a system may work over a short period of time, but it will never develop a flow of competent executives from bottom to top; nor will it develop a happy, enthusiastic team.

On the other hand, when authority is delegated, there can be no long periods of delay waiting for decisions to be made by those who have accepted responsibility. Therefore, top management must always be available to discuss the problems of young executives with them in an atmosphere in which arguments are encouraged and prolonged to bring out the facts. Always, the discussion should be pointed to the final decision being made by the responsible executive and not by top management. This can be done if the contacts between the various echelons of management are frequent and informal. If such contacts do not exist, then it is time for the chairman of the board to get out of his chair and visit his young executives to create the relationships favorable to informal discussion.

All my life I have heard of the executive who has so cleared his desk and arranged his schedule that he has no details to worry about and can devote all his time to what is called long-range planning. I suppose there are such executives somewhere. The only ones I know personally who have reached this condition have long lost their ability either to administer or to think. The chief executive who is vitally interested in the growth of his company, and in the development of its personnel, must do his thinking at home or on weekends because his spare working hours will be occupied in seeing the young executives who come to him or in going to those who do not come to him.

Responsibility can be delegated with the requisite grant of authorily to permit its exercise. However, the ultimate responsibility for placing responsibility in proper hands and the supervision required to determine the extent and degree to which delegation is effective can never be delegated. The chief executive whose company continues to grow will seldom be found in his office; he will be visiting not only within his office but also in field offices and plants.

Through such visits he begins to know the individuals who form the team, to find out if communication from top to bottom is effective, to determine those within the executive chain who have capacities for growth. No man can be judged fairly through another man's eyes; no man can be judged better than in the exercise of responsibility at his place of work. Moreover, a competent chief executive will find that with each visit to a plant or office the feel of the job and the information which he obtains have added value. The formality of first acquaintance has been overcome. Junior executives have become willing to talk freely and informally, eager to express their thoughts and ideas on how the company can improve. These talks must never lead to criticism of others; rather they must be led into discussions of company policies and procedures. It is surprising how stimulating these field trips can become to the chief executive who makes them a part of his duties.

I regret that I must resort to personal experience to convey my thoughts and ideas with respect to organization. Please do not think that in doing so I am posing as a particularly competent and able manager. I do make it a practice to visit each of our 80-odd plants at least once a year, and on these visits to sit down with the plant managers and sales managers at luncheons or dinners when possible. I cannot say that our plant and sales managers find these visits helpful; but I do say that if I did not make these visits, I could not perform my responsibilities because I have no other way to know the people who are really responsible for the profits earned by our company.

Also, the chief executive who visits the field regularly sets the pattern for other executives. This develops the personal knowledge and relationships throughout the organization which make it more of a team than it would be otherwise. Moreover, these visits make it possible for ways to be found to help the young executives. No one can say how a senior executive can help a particular junior executive, for such help can succeed only as it is fitted to both personalities.

Some young men assuming executive power are overzealous in exerting authority, too eager to make decisions without discussion with others — to demonstrate their executive courage. Often they are too aggressive in argument to allow their own assistants the opportunity to be heard. In some instances, the reins must be applied sharply and quickly. In others, men entering into higher executive positions have the basic information and knowledge which they need but lack the confidence of experience and are unwilling to back their own judgments against those of associates who appear to be more mature and to have more experience. Here it is essential to draw out fully the views of the new executive, and to support him while he is gaining the confidence to maintain his position and in such a way that he never realizes the help which he is receiving.

Still young executives will come to your office to place their problem before you to decide. In such cases, the discussion must be directed to confirm their views and draw from them the decision which they were unwilling to make for themselves. After a few such experiences, the visits become fewer and decisions are made at the proper place. Sometimes this lack of confidence comes from too much stress on errors in judgment which lead to bad decisions. Although errors in judgment cannot be permitted to go unnoticed, there are many ways in which they can be pointed out without condemnation. In our organization, it is somewhat of an axiom that while you must live with your own errors, the only unforgivable failure is the failure to make a decision or to do the things which must be done.

Once again referring to personal experiences, I was fortunate in the Army in working under several outstanding executives who have proved themselves in other fields. When General Somervell was designated to set up the Services of Supply, he advised me that I was being assigned to him as the Director of Resources and Requirements. I asked, "What does this mean?" and his reply was, "Your job is to find out what the Army needs to fight with, and then see that it is produced." That, indeed, proved to be my job, and I do not think that I ever had any other charter. However, General Somervell installed a control system which kept him fully informed on progress so that he could exercise the supervision essential to successful delegation of responsibility.

Subsequently, I became Deputy Military Governor of Germany under General Eisenhower, which again was a new and unknown field. My headquarters was in Berlin, while General Eisenhower remained in Frankfurt. He gave me full responsibility for the establishment of military government. However, each week he would visit me in Berlin for a full day, most of which would be devoted to general discussion of occupation problems and policies. So informal and broad were these discussions that it never occurred to me then, nor could I state now, from which of us came the major decisions which determined our course of action in Germany. In discussion we reached the mutuality of viewpoint which is the ideal relationship between senior and junior in any organization.

Those two men realized what so many never grasp: that the strong man never hesitates to delegate authority, and never loses patience because difficulties arise, as long as the responsible executive is taking adequate measures to cope with such difficulties.

The human touch at the right time is of equal importance. General Patton drove his corps and division commanders hard, setting high standards and demanding meticulous performance. In point of fact, in quiet moments his subordinate generals were sometimes not too happy to have him arrive for a visit. However, General Paul tells this story of a visit which his division received from General Patton:

> Paul, moving rapidly, suddenly found his division some miles to the front of the divisions on his right and left. Faced with heavy German resistance which included attacks on both flanks, the going was tough. At its toughest moment General Patton arrived at the division command post. Paul said to himself as he went out to meet Patton, "Haven't I got enough of a problem on my hands now not to be bawled out, too, for being in this predicament?"
>
> As they came together Patton threw his arm about Paul's shoulders and said, "Stew, my boy, you've got enough problems to solve today without being bothered by me. You will take care of them; but if you need any help, let me know. Good-bye." With this, Patton climbed back in his car and left. In those few words he had strengthened Paul's confidence to master the situation.

Every executive will have comparable situations with his assistants; and if he knows them as individuals, he will instinctively find the right approach to maintain their confidence. Likewise, he would recognize instantly if the man on the job, unlike Paul, did not have the equipment and ability to meet the situation and so needed to be replaced on the spot to prevent disaster.

Another important factor to sound understanding which can never be overdone is the ability to give the responsible executives full credit for the results which follow the exercise of good judgment. You can be proud of the credit, which is rightfully yours, that he has such competent assistants. Any executive who is deeply interested in his organization often resorts to the planting of ideas among his immediate assistants so that, as those ideas develop into reality, credit for both the idea and its execution may be given to these assistants. No opportunity should be lost to place each executive in the line of authority in favorable light to those who work for him, and to his associates.

While I have referred to the desirability of informal discussions at frequent intervals as a sound approach to proper human relationships, informality should never become the order of the day. That quality which we call discipline in the Army, and which may be better described perhaps as the maintenance of dignified relationships among the individuals and elements of an organization, is fundamental to a successful organization. Informal discussions should not become back-slapping.

Perhaps one of the most difficult things to learn in life is that, as we proceed up the ladder, we can no longer be a part and parcel of the lowest rung. There is a dignity of position to maintain. It does not come from being aloof, nor from avoiding past associations. It cannot be held by winning a popularity contest. It is a natural product of growth upward. If it does not result, then the growth which brought about the upward move was apparent and not real. This is not an easy concept. Too frequently, it develops the stuffed shirt executive and creates a stilted artificial atmosphere around him.

Business can be fun; in fact it must be fun for those who are working together if the maximum effort is to result. It can be fun only when relationships are informal and easy, but with subconscious recognition of the worth of those who occupy high executive office and respect for the abilities which have earned them their positions.

Sometimes I am asked how problems can be discussed properly with junior executives on field visits which they have not as yet discussed with their immediate superiors. Personally, I find no difficulty in discussing with them, and in considerable detail, any company problem with which they are concerned without committing myself—asking questions and developing points of view which may help them in a better presentation of their views through appropriate channels. It is made clear that the problem is being probed, not decided. In point of fact, these discussions often concern problems that are solved in the field and never reach the head office.

I must admit that I have not discussed the art of delegation in precise or concise terms and that I have failed to lay down any rules to be followed in determining how and to whom to delegate responsibility. If I have minimized the importance of the organization charts and of the position analyses which form the basis for organization, it is because the principles which govern their presentation are well established. They are contained in the textbooks written by management experts and seem relatively easy to apply to any business. If that were all that was necessary to ensure a sound organization, then delegation would be a science and not an art.

Once again I repeat that an organization is a collection of individuals and that the relationships which exist among these individuals will be the determining factor in its success. Since these relationships depend so much on the individual, let us examine a few qualities which the executive needs to possess:

Each executive in the chain must know his job to be able to subdivide and delegate his responsibilities.

He must know the individuals to whom he is giving authority to be sure that it is within their capacity, or to be sure that he can develop their capacity to exercise it properly.

He must have a constant flow of statistical information to his desk to enable him to measure the performance of those to whom he has delegated authority.

He must visit them frequently to judge their performance on the job and how they in turn are delegating authority and developing subordinates who will be capable of accepting further responsibilities.

He must hold down the brash without destroying their confidence, draw out the timid without making their decisions, give credit to those who deserve it, take the blame for those who fail until repeated failure has demonstrated their unworthiness, be patient when judgments prove wrong, and be angry and impatient only when mishaps occur because decisions have not been made.

He must be accessible to all who work under him, sufficiently free in his relationships to have their confidence; and yet he must maintain an indefinable reserve — a dignity of position consistent with that wise old axiom "familiarity breeds contempt."

To do all this, he must be the master of the position he occupies and be fully informed about the progress of the activities under his direction. He must be the buffer between his organization and the public; and he must earn and hold a reputation and a public standing which entitle him to the respect of his associates.

If he is and can do these things, then indeed he can fit the chart to the individual, or the individual to the chart, with the flexibility that turns an organization on paper into an effective management team. Perhaps there has yet been no complete master of management, no one who fully understands the art of delegation. But the complexities of modern management have given to those of us who exercise management far better tools to work with than we have had in the past; and increasingly there is evidence of a growing understanding of the importance of human relationships to the success of any organization.

Certainly, as one proceeds upward in a management career, his real satisfaction comes from looking at the organization and finding within it the men in whom he has placed his confidence growing in capacity and rising to new challenges.

If I could conclude with one thought that has been most helpful to me in delegating responsibility and in granting authority, that thought would be: the executive must know his people, for only in that knowledge can he approach with hope of success the selection of those to exercise authority. If he has selected them properly, he will find it almost impossible to retain the authorities and responsibilities which he should have given up long ago.

MANAGEMENT COMMUNICATION

*Elmer L. Lindseth**

This chapter deals with communication, which like delegation and control (the subjects discussed in the preceding and the following chapters) is one of the important words in today's management vocabulary. Just where does communication fit in today's picture? What part does communication play in releasing the full potential of the management team?

By now there is no question that effective delegation is *essential* to releasing that full potential. But is a workable system of delegation *possible* without good communication? Will the decentralized executive—the delegatee—be able to perform effectively if he lacks essential information? Or if his efforts are not co-ordinated with—that is, communicated to—other delegatees? Or if he does not feed back effectively? The prospect is doubtful.

In the field of measurement and control, similar questions arise. Without fresh and reliable information can we measure performance of a delegated function? Without means of speedily and accurately getting executive decisions and policy to the level of delegation can a delegator know that operations will go as intended? Without good communication upward can a delegator know enough of what is going on at the level of delegation so that he in his ivory tower may make sound decisions? Again, it is extremely doubtful.

We all communicate, adequately or inadequately, efficiently or inefficiently, throughout the working day. A study of the executive working pattern by the Dutch management consultant, Luijk,

* Mr. Lindseth, who gave the address on which this chapter is based, is President of The Cleveland Electric Illuminating Company. Starting as a test helper in 1924, he became successively junior tester, production engineer, assistant to the executive engineer, technical assistant to the president, assistant to the president, vice president, and executive vice president, assuming his present position in 1945.

reveals that 60 per cent of an executive's time is devoted to communication in one form or another. So there should be little question about the *importance* of communication.

Nor is there much question of the extent of *interest* in communication and its problems. There is a vast literature on communication. Discussions of communication are frequent at meetings and at conferences like the one this book is based on. Considerable research is going on in the field. Scientists have reduced it to mathematical theory; they have even demonstrated that all the information communicated by a man in his entire lifetime, if properly and efficiently encoded, could be transmitted over a modern television channel in 10 seconds. Engineers have reduced the communication process to graphs and diagrams. Psychologists also have worked hard at it.

But although communication is in one sense commonplace, and its study widespread, it is not simple—far from it. In fact, communication is so difficult that Professor Roethlisberger has said: "In thinking about the many barriers to personal communication, particularly those that are due to differences of background, experience, and motivation, it seems to me extraordinary that any two persons can ever understand each other." [1]

So in communication we find an interesting paradox. Here is something we do a very large portion of the time, something vitally important, yet apparently extremely difficult to do successfully.

And here again we are setting about considering this universal problem, which is so frequently discussed, which is so often written about, and which we work at every day. "There's nothing new under the sun," we are told. Even so, let us see if we can distill something which, while it may not add much to what the specialists know, should provide some ideas that most businessmen can use in their relations with their associates.

Most readers will be familiar with the many techniques of management communication: (a) the use of conferences, seminars, breakfast meetings, luncheon meetings, dinner meetings, reviews,

[1] Carl R. Rogers and F. J. Roethlisberger, "Barriers and Gateways to Communication," *Harvard Business Review,* July-August 1952, p. 50.

résumés, and the myriad other means of oral communication; (b) the use of policy manuals, bulletins, newsletters, pamphlets, graphs, performance letters, reports, and the thousand-and-one means of written management communication; and (c) the use of counseling and informal face-to-face and telephone techniques which supply so much intramanagement communication.

The literature and discussions are replete with rules and techniques of effective communication. Dr. Rudolf Flesch has boiled down his recommendations for easily readable written communication to a few simple precepts:

1. Avoid long sentences.
2. Avoid the abstract word, the legalistic word, and the two-dollar word.
3. Shorten sentences to an average of 17 words.
4. Shorten words to an average of 150 syllables per 100 words.
5. Use about 6 personal references per 100 words.[2]

Dr. Robert Shurter of Case Institute of Technology has also given us five rules to ensure clarity in written communication (note how much easier it is to be specific about writing than speaking):

1. Fix the responsibility for clarity firmly on the writer.
2. Remember the reader — avoid jargon and the vocabulary of the specialist.
3. Let it be known that you are not impressed by length.
4. Have each document begin with a concise statement of what it is about.
5. Let those who report to you know how you want the information organized.[3]

I could cite other sets of "simple" rules. But can it be as easy as it looks?

If it is, why are so many people in management uninformed? Why are top executives so isolated and so insulated? Why, in our system of delegation, which General Clay describes, do our delegatees

[2] Rudolf Flesch, *The Art of Readable Writing* (New York, Harper & Brothers, 1949).

[3] Robert L. Shurter, "Techniques for Improving Written Communications," an address before a meeting of the Case Associates, Case Institute of Technology, May 13, 1954.

make decisions and take actions without the knowledge of other people who also ought to participate in them? Why, under our system of delegation, do situations sneak up on the delegator which "he thought" were taken care of? In short, why does our ideal of delegation and control so often get fouled up?

We are forced to the unhappy conclusion that the basic communication problem is not entirely one of techniques. There must be more to it than that.

We find that for the effective application of the techniques of communication, there is need of what is variously described as a proper "climate," or proper "conditions" — a proper "atmosphere" and the proper "attitudes" — on the part of those engaged in communication.

These conditions precedent to the establishment of good communication are not to be taken for granted. They are, in fact, rarely present; something keeps them from being easily achieved. For want of a better term, let us regard these factors other than the conventional techniques as comprising the philosophy of communication.

Soon it becomes clearer why — when communication is so universally necessary, when we have this great body of literature on the subject, when we have all these simple techniques — it is still so difficult to communicate effectively. Probably the main reason is that communication is a human function conducted by and between human beings, and no two human beings are alike. John M. McCaffery, the president of the International Harvester Company, put it concisely in *Fortune* several months ago: "The biggest problem with industry is that it is full of human beings."[4]

The language used in discussing communication is replete with negatives: the "difficulties" of communication, the "blocks," the "obstacles," the "barriers." "Noise" also is a word with special semantic meaning in communication. Let us list these barriers — these negatives — and examine them briefly.

Barrier No. 1 to good communication, it seems to me, is the *lack*

[4] John M. McCaffery, "What Corporation Presidents Think About at Night," *Fortune*, September 1953, p. 128.

of a proper climate of confidence and mutual understanding. People in management have different backgrounds, different objectives, different ambitions, and different motivations. These differences make for a tremendous variation in perspective among members of the management group. Each executive deals with communication in a different context: each evaluates any situation which requires communication between him and others with a purely personal frame of reference.

In practice, this variation in perspective is frequently complicated by the lack of a sense of common purpose in the management group. People whose goals, as well as backgrounds, are different—people who are not united through working to achieve a common purpose—find themselves communicating at cross-purposes. All too frequently they think they are talking about one thing when in fact they are talking about two entirely different things. Presumably the subject is the same to both, but divergent personal concepts of the subject—different evaluations not only of the subject but of what the other fellow means by the subject—preclude the possibility of really effective understanding.

A little experiment (modeled on one they use at Massachusetts Institute of Technology) may point up the difficulty of communicating without a common frame of reference:

> Suppose I say, "A man was walking along. He looked down at his suit and saw a hole in it. In a minute he was dead."
>
> What picture comes into your mind? What did I communicate to you?
>
> If I led you to the conclusion that the man was walking along a street, that the hole was a bullet hole, and that he died of the wound, you have reached the conclusion of the vast majority. You are normal. But your conclusion is not what I intended.
>
> Actually, the facts are these: the man was a deep-sea diver; he was walking on the ocean bottom; the hole was in his diving suit; he died by drowning.

Each of us translated this little story in terms of his own frame of reference. It is easy to see how different the results can be. I communicated the information in one context, you the reader received it in another, and certainly we failed to achieve effective communication.

Another important aspect of this barrier is *prestige* and its companion, *fear*. The boss, the top man—whoever the figure may be behind the traditionally open door—receives upward communication that has been filtered and conditioned by the prestige he bears. Who likes to bring bad news to the boss?

Prestige and fear operate at every level. Much voluntary communication is suppressed because of subordinate reaction to ordinary fear. That is why so many good ideas die at the boss's threshold. Fear of disapproval—an unwanted sentry—effectively closes the open door.

So the first requirement of effective communication is a climate of confidence and mutual understanding.

Barrier No. 2 in my listing is the *lack of motivation to communicate*. This particular obstacle arises often where there is no sound tradition of good communication.

In the first place, one who is himself the victim of poor communication will not have too much material to communicate. Secondly, he is not stimulated by precept and example to attempt to communicate efficiently. Thirdly, he is often insecure. Imperfect knowledge of the situation, combined with a lack of confidence or security, tends to make him draw in his horns, play it close to the vest. The less he communicates, the fewer mistakes he can make, or at least be charged with. He is the familiar guy who will not stick his neck out so they cannot hang something on him.

This lack of the desire or will to communicate is usually due to lack of motivation and is bound up with the previous obstacle, absence of the proper climate of confidence. While the desire to communicate rarely exists without this necessary climate, the reverse is not true. Mere creation of the proper communication climate will not guarantee creation of the desire to communicate. But it is a prerequisite.

An example of this is found in the report of a management firm which had been requested to install a personnel department in a company that had existed without one for years. In studying the firm, the consultants found that the president had isolated himself both physically and communicatively from the rest of the organization. His example provided no motivation to other executives to communicate. After study, the consultants concluded that their real job was not to set up a personnel department — which would have had to operate in a vacuum — but to establish a sound communication pattern in the company.

So the second requirement is to create the desire — the will — among our people to communicate.

Barrier No. 3 I list as the *failure to realize the emotional and psychological nature of communication* — the mistaken assumption that communication is something essentially logical. It may not be logical at all. It may be basically the conveying of the emotional reaction of one man to another. This has no necessary connection with logic.

Take the case of the hunch or — as it is called in the higher echelons — executive intuition. Many decisions are made on this basis. But the hunch itself, or the intuition, is not a logical thing, and is almost impossible to communicate or explain with accuracy and efficiency.

It is a false assumption that words in themselves, apart from the people involved, have meaning. Words are mere symbols that mean one thing in one situation and something else in another, or one thing when used by one man and something quite different when used by another. From time to time we find ourselves in the plight of the furniture dealer who had a delinquent account of long standing:

> After trying various approaches, he decided on an appeal to pride. "What will your neighbors think," he wrote, "when our truck backs up to your house and we repossess your furniture?"
>
> There was a delay of several days before he got his answer: "I have asked my neighbors and they all think it would be a lousy, low-down trick."

So the third requirement is to realize how tough and tricky this communication job is.

Barrier No. 4 is the *failure to listen intelligently.* Often when we do listen, we listen with our ears but not with our minds. We listen to words, but we do not translate words into meaning.

Isolated as we are, each with his unique frame of reference, we make judgments and evaluations when communication is thrust upon us. But we do so without having listened intelligently. We have not tried to put ourselves in the other fellow's place, to see the subject as he sees it, and, consequently, to understand what it means to him and what he is trying to say to us. This failure to listen intelligently has blighted more communication than we dream of in our wildest imaginings.

So the fourth requirement is to listen with our minds as well as with our ears.

Barrier No. 5 is a corollary to the previous one: ***our failure to measure the effectiveness of our communication,*** to determine what is getting through. The engineers refer to this as a lack of "feedback."

We communicate—or we believe that we communicate—but, without measurement, without feedback, we have no means of evaluating the efficiency of our communication. We sit back, believing that we have communicated well. Better feedback would shatter this complacency and expose our inadequacy. We might even be stimulated to try again, to try for really good communication.

The college professor, who has been working at this problem a long time, has a highly developed system of feedback. During the week he lectures, he communicates. But come Friday he measures the efficiency of his communication with a quiz. Here is the feedback which shatters his blissful complacency and stimulates him to try again—to try to communicate the same simple facts to the same simple minds. There is a lesson here for all of us.

We hear it said that communication is a two-way street. This principle is more important than we think. To illustrate:

Professor Alex Bavelas of M. I. T. placed two people in separate rooms. The first was given a telephone by which he could send messages to the second, who could listen but had no way of talking back. The sender was then given a blank piece of paper with several small blocks placed on it in random fashion. The listener was given a similar piece of paper and the same number of blocks. The object of the experiment was to have the listener arrange the blocks on his paper in the same pattern as the sender's. The sender was free to describe locations of the blocks in any way he wished, such as number of inches from the border, and so on. But the communication was one way only. In not a single case, it is reported, was the listener successful in getting all the blocks properly placed.

A one-way communication system such as this has little chance of succeeding because there is no feedback.

So the fifth requirement for successful communication is simply to know what is getting through.

Barrier No. 6—the first of a group of barriers which presuppose at least an organized attempt at communication, and perhaps some success—is the *failure to emphasize and encourage the three-way nature of communication.* Often we hear that communication must be from the top down and from the bottom up. Both are vital. No less important, as many have pointed out, is lateral communication—the interchange of information and ideas, not from one echelon of authority to another, but horizontally through each echelon.

Without effective *downward* communication, policies, philosophies, decisions, orders, and information cannot be brought to the action level at the proper time and in the proper form. Top management decisions stagnate at the top, and all those on lower echelons remain in isolation. Without good *upward* communication, insufficient facts and results reach the level of policy decision. This produces executive isolation—the ivory-tower effect—and leads to the fatal process of making decisions in a vacuum.

Without voluntary *lateral* communication, there is no co-ordination or integration of the efforts of every manager in the organization. Only through effective lateral communication can different elements in the organization co-ordinate their efforts. Differences frankly exposed, in a process which Mary Parker Follett called "constructive conflict," are a healthy sign.[5] This process must take place at every level. But too infrequently do we find it.

[5] Henry C. Metcalf and L. Urwick, Editors, *Dynamic Administration: The Collected Papers of Mary Parker Follett* (New York, Harper & Brothers, 1941), p. 30.

Let me quote from Peter Drucker:

"The mass-production technology demands an integration of the individual operation into a unified whole. It is this whole, the team, the pattern, the organization, which produces in the modern industrial system. This 'whole' does not exist in the individual operations themselves . . . The very strength and functioning of the enterprise may well depend on the attainment of a 'managerial attitude' by the middle groups. These groups are the organization itself, the nerve and circulatory system of the enterprise.

"Unlike their ancestors the skilled artisan, supervision, middle management and technicians need no skill in the handling of tools or of materials. Their 'skill' is the ability to integrate. They have to fit the work of their department into their own work. Top management can set the pattern, but middle management and supervision must live it." [6]

So the sixth requirement, if we would have good communication in our outfit, is to encourage and practice horizontal as well as vertical communication.

Barrier No. 7 often exists even within a well-thought-out communication structure: *failure to use the most expeditious communication channels.* This stems from the old conflict of channels of contact and channels of authority.

The formal pattern of communication usually follows the organizational pattern of the business, and thus flows through channels of authority. Far more necessary, however, is an effective informal pattern of communication which flows through channels of contact — through which the man who needs a piece of information gets it directly from the man who has it. The difference between the two is the difference between getting things done the easy way, and getting them done in the "old army way." (I am told that the new army way recognizes this problem.)

Since normally these two sets of channels are entirely different, some people sense conflict in their simultaneous existence. Some feel that communication outside the formal channels of authority leads to a loss of control. This is the viewpoint of the typical poor communicator and the insecure.

[6] Peter Drucker, *The New Society; The Anatomy of the Industrial Order* (New York, Harper & Brothers, 1950), p. 158.

Poles apart from this is the attitude of the General Electric Company, expressed in a footnote to its organization chart, which I quote:

"Channels of Contact. While the organization structure and chart define lines of responsibility, authority, and accountability, they do not indicate or limit CHANNELS OF CONTACT, OR FLOW OF INFORMATION, between or among members of the organization. Organization policy permits and expects the exercise of common sense and good judgment, at all organization levels, in determining the best channels of contact for expeditious handling of Company work. Contacts, and flow of information, between people and components of the organization should be carried out in the simplest and most direct way practicable . . ."

A lot of thought and experience went into that footnote. It is worth the serious consideration of all of us.

So the seventh requirement is to avoid getting bogged down in channels.

Barrier No. 8 is the *failure to apply successful known communication techniques.* There is not much excuse for this. It is almost the case of the farmer resisting change—not buying something that will improve his methods because he does not farm now half as well as he knows how to.

We have referred to the great amount of study and research that has been done on communication. There are tried and tested techniques for almost any situation, and they fit the needs of virtually any business organization. It is our responsibility to select the proper techniques for our own particular circumstances and to see that they work. This is not easy, but it is essential.

Part of the trouble is the failure to provide regular and routine mechanisms to expedite the flow of communication. Staff meetings, performance analysis meetings, supervisors' meetings—whatever forms of regular face-to-face communication are used—fill a real need. Each enterprise must develop its own routines.

But whether the communication mechanisms be written or oral, regular scheduling is a big help. Meetings at a set time each day or week or month, reports or newsletters on a prescribed timetable, are immensely helpful. While this sounds like a gimmick, it is well worth while.

So the eighth requirement is to learn and use the established techniques, the well-known rules. But learning is a slow process, as illustrated by the plight of the poor fellow with the broken arm:

For years, he explained, he had been accustomed to sneaking downstairs for a midnight snack from the refrigerator.

His dog habitually slept at the foot of the stairs. Over the years he had stepped on the dog's tail, his ears, and his paws.

But this night he stepped right on Rover's belly. The dog rolled over, yelping, and our friend took a spectacular tumble, breaking his arm.

"Now wouldn't you think," he asked, "after all these years that the damn dog would have learned something?"

Barrier No. 9, the last on my list, is the *failure to take the mystery out of communication.* Through all the work that has been done, and through all that has been written about communication, a great aura of mystery and emotion has sprung up.

Harold Smiddy of General Electric offers a practical solution. "A great deal could be accomplished," he says, "if we would consider communication in the light of this simple, four-word formula: 'Talk to the guy!' "

While communication is not quite that simple, the formula has much to recommend it. So if we "talk to the guy," if we always tell him *why,* we may do away with some of the false mystery cloaking the subject, and thus allow ourselves to come to grips with the kernel of the matter instead of wasting our strength and efforts in fighting phantoms.

So, then, the ninth and final requirement is to go at the problem simply and straightforwardly.

There is a very negative feeling to the consideration of so many obstacles to effective communication. Still, it is necessary to think of them.

What we are trying to do here is to find a constructive pattern which will help us in solving our communication problems or, at the very least, will give us a start toward that highly desirable end. This pattern must take into consideration all the barriers that we have mentioned and must offer some hope for a final solution.

We are not going to build Rome in a day. There is no simple

panacea for this complex problem. There is, however, much of a constructive nature that we can do. We can define and resolve to bring about in our own organizations or in our own individual spheres of responsibility, however small or large, the conditions precedent for the establishment of a truly efficient communication pattern.

In doing this, we must recognize first and foremost that we can do little about the innate differences between human beings. But a community of interest, acceptance of the team spirit, and identification of an individual's goals with those of his organization will do a job — albeit perhaps less than a 100 per cent job — of reducing those subjective differences in the matter of communication.

We can do much to establish a healthy communication atmosphere by precept and example. Certainly all of us can listen more and better. We can instill in those we contact the desire and willingness to communicate. We can help those responsible to us to master the basic skills of clear expression and the ability to listen intelligently to others in order to receive meanings rather than words.

While making a start on these — and I believe that we all realize how long and hard a task it will be — we may apply those effective techniques of communication best fitted to the needs of our particular organizations.

When we have done all this, we shall have taken at least one long stride down the road to better communication.

Thus, we have covered a lot of discouraging material, and we have come out at the end with a hard task before us. So long as we realize the magnitude of that task, so long as we are willing to work hard and long to accomplish it, our feet are on the right path, and I for one believe that we can succeed in the end.

And when we succeed, what shall we accomplish? As we bring our communication up to a level of even reasonable effectiveness, we shall enable ourselves to do what General Clay in the preceding chapter points up as being so highly desirable — namely, to achieve some order of effective delegation. Further, we shall make possible co-ordination and integration at the level of delegation. We shall also provide tools for obtaining better performance reporting, better performance measurement, and control, which Mr. Yntema describes in the following chapter.

In short, we shall find, as we approach truly effective communication, that we have realized one of the three necessary steps in releasing the full potential of the management team.

But—let me emphasize—while there is a way out of our communication problems, there is no *easy* way out. No single approach is a cure-all. Above all, we must not let communication remain in the cloudland of theory. We must apply our efforts, maybe not with blood, but certainly with sweat and possibly with tears. We must work and work some more until our own communication problems are, if not cured, at least rendered less acute.

As leaders, it is up to us at all times to set the proper example. Words are never enough. John Riegel puts it this way: "The force of example is the most effective single means of communication."[7] St. Matthew said: "By their fruits ye shall know them."

Now I do not want to sound naive. Our problems are universal. They are present in big corporations and in little ones. But a formula composed of intelligence, some of the thoughts we have discussed here, and a tremendous amount of hard work will get us started.

The Book of Revelation says: "Behold, I have set before thee an open door . . ."

[7] John W. Riegel, "How You Can Do Your Management Job Better," an address before the Cleveland Electric Illuminating Company Management Group, April 27, 1954.

MEASUREMENT AND CONTROL

*By Theodore O. Yntema**

Measurement and control are concepts for the philosopher. Within their scope I shall deal with a somewhat more specific, though still very large, subject — a system of controls in business. Such a system is not easy to characterize briefly. If the system is full-fledged, it embodies the major policies of the business; it is a working program for the future; it reveals the financial consequences of alternatives *before* major decisions are made; and it provides means for coordinating and integrating various plans and activities into an efficient operation.

Most, if not all, important ideas are simple — often deceptively so. The conversion of mass into energy can be described in a simple equation; yet its applications are bewildering and its results terrifying. The economic propositions that have general validity would fill only a few pages; yet the maze of economic interactions baffles the forecasters. Coming closer to home, the fundamentals of counting, order, measurement, classification, and tabulation seem so elementary that beginners sometimes turn up their noses in sophomoric scorn. But only you with actual experience know what incredible thought and work go into the construction of a good system of controls in business.

After reviewing the literature and thinking back over my experience, I have tried to pick out some ideas that seem to me simple and important. They are not as fundamental as physical laws, economic propositions, or principles of classification, but they have

* Mr. Yntema, who gave the address on which this chapter is based, is Vice President–Finance, Ford Motor Company, having joined the company in 1949. He had previously been Professor of Statistics, and later Professor of Business and Economic Policy, at the University of Chicago. He was Research Director of the Committee for Economic Development until 1949.

helped me, and I hope they will be of some use to you. I shall address myself to two questions:

A. What are the essential conditions for a system of business controls to operate effectively?
B. Why is such a system needed in business?

What are the essential conditions for a system of business controls to operate effectively?

(1) I should list foremost the role of top management—its active participation and leadership. Here there are three points:

(a) Certain fundamental policies of top management must be expressed and embodied in the system of controls. These include policies in regard to profit objectives, pricing, production schedules, facility planning, and financial planning.
(b) Top management must take the time needed to give careful, intelligent review to the plans of profit center managers and to follow up on variance of performance from approved plans.
(c) Top management must make it clear that rewards in salary, bonus, promotion, and commendation are based primarily on performance.

The controller (or the head of the planning and control staff if he is elsewhere in the organization) must be a master technician and psychologist—but he is *not* the real controller of the business. That is the job of the president—shared in some cases with the executive committee. No control system can work without the leadership and active participation of top management.

(2) If the control system is to be directed toward making profits—as it must—a company of any size and diversity should be subdivided into profit centers. The manager of each profit center should have the responsibility and necessary authority to operate his division as a separate business, subject only to general guidance from broad company policies and, on critical decisions, review by top management. Some of the advantages of such decentralization are fairly obvious: it increases the proportion of important executives charged directly with the responsibility for making a profit; it reduces in size and complexity the individual profit-making unit; and it brings the profit-seeking manager closer to actual operations.

Not quite so obvious are the incentive to economize in the use of assets and the stimulus to seek additional sources of revenue.

(3) A control system must look to the future. The heart of such a system is forecasting — the projection of business plans and alternatives into the future. Study of the past is useful, but analysis and evaluation of the results of actions *before* they are taken provide the real foundations for wise decisions.

(4) A highly competent staff is needed to develop and operate a system of controls. Although the leadership and authority for decisions must come from top management, the president obviously cannot deal with the myriad of problems arising from day to day in profit-center accounting and forecasting. He must look to his staff in such matters — probably to his controller.

While the technical work of planning and control may be done in a separate staff office, there are important advantages in combining it with the controller's other functions. Many of the forecasts are projections of accounting data. Moreover, the unification of accounting, financial analysis, and related controls in one office at the central staff level can be paralleled by a corresponding combination in the divisions. This simplifies the functional relations between staff and divisions — relations which are none too easy to maintain on a mutually satisfactory basis.

The key technician in a system of controls — hereafter I shall call him the controller — has a demanding and difficult job. In my judgment few people are equipped to handle such a job in a large, complicated business. Some of the problems are technical and hard to solve, and the sheer volume of them is likely to overwhelm most men. Moreover, as our controller is wont to say to me, "The technical problems may be tough — but the really important part of our job is people." Understanding of people, fairness, and integrity are just as necessary qualifications for the controller and his staff as technical ability, capacity, and drive.

To my first question, then, "What are the essential conditions for a system of controls to operate effectively?" I have given four answers:

1. The leadership and active participation of top management.

2. The establishment of profit centers (if the business is of substantial size and complexity).

3. The use of forecasting, i.e., business projections, as a working tool of management.

4. A controller and associated staff of high competence, integrity, and ability to get along with people.

My second question, "Why is a system of controls needed in business?" can be answered simply.

(1) Most people work harder and better if they have definite goals which have been accepted by all concerned.

(2) Since the goals, i.e., the standards or budgets, are regularly re-examined, there is constant search for means to raise standards and improve performance.

(3) Detailed planning and integration of various activities lead to a better co-ordinated operation.

(4) Since the results of programs and decisions are forecasted, it is possible to catch many mistakes before they are made and to take steps to remedy situations that promise to be unsatisfactory.

(5) Although a system of controls requires the active participation of top management, it makes possible greater delegation of authority and responsibility and less routine supervision. Thus, more top management time is freed for constructive action.

(6) A proper system of controls focuses the efforts of management on making profits. I believe the profit motivation in business needs strengthening. Many executives, I suspect, are not quite as interested in making a dollar for the business as in making a dollar for themselves — especially an after-tax dollar. This dilution of the profit motive results from taxation, from the separation of ownership and management, and from division of work and specialization. In part, this situation can be remedied by profit bonuses and stock options. Even these will not hold in line the natural propensities toward bigger and better things in each special phase of the business. Yet the biggest advertising campaigns, the newest factories, the most magnificent engineering establishment, the most advanced industrial relations, the greatest in public relations, and the most comprehensive system of records and reports

will not add up to the most profits for the company. These special interests can be held in balance only by careful budget reviews, by decentralizing activities to profit centers insofar as is practicable, and by the constant pressures from profit-responsible executives who ultimately have to pay the bill.

To recapitulate: A system of controls is needed in business because it helps to bring about better work, more efforts for improvement, and more effective co-ordination of activities. Through systematic forecasts it reduces mistakes. By increasing the possibilities of delegation, it frees top executive time for constructive work. And, finally, but by no means least, it strengthens the profit motivation in business.

PART II

EFFECTIVE DELEGATION AND CONTROL BY THE GENERAL MANAGER

In an Atomic Energy Commission Plant

*By Albert J. Gracia**

In my discussion of this subject, it must be recognized that the situation of the Goodyear Atomic Corporation is at least unusual, if not unique. A short time ago our corporation was formed by Goodyear Tire & Rubber Company, as a wholly owned subsidiary, to operate the billion-dollar gaseous diffusion plant under construction in the Portsmouth, Ohio, area. This tremendous industrial complex is designed to produce fissionable uranium for the needs of the nation, both for defense purposes and for the peacetime application of nuclear energy.

The gaseous diffusion process is an incredibly complicated, continuous manufacturing operation, involving the processing of large quantities of expensive uranium compounds which must always be maintained in the system under strict analytical control, constant security surveillance, and ready accountability.

Let me comment about this accountability. We have to account for the total uranium inventory at all times. How difficult this is can be seen from the fact that several months must elapse from the day we start pumping material into the system until the product emerges at the end of the line. So, with a hold-up time (as the engineers say) of some months, we must always be ready to account for the entire inventory of uranium compounds to the Atomic Control Commission. This involves a force of something like 70

* Mr. Gracia is General Manager, Goodyear Atomic Corporation. He went into research and development work for Goodyear Tire & Rubber Company in 1928, subsequently becoming assistant to the vice president in charge of research and development, and moving to his present position with Goodyear Atomic Corporation when that subsidiary was formed some two years ago.

people, among them analysts, business machine operators, engineers, and clerical assistants.

The plant is operated under a contract with the Atomic Energy Commission, which contract spells out in detail the degree of the operating contractor's responsibility, liability, and reimbursability. A Commission office is maintained at the Portsmouth site, with an area manager and a staff to administer the contracts of the prime contractors, both construction and operating. Besides Goodyear Atomic Corporation and the Atomic Energy Commission, there are presently on the site the prime construction contractor, Peter Kiewit & Sons; Kiewit's subcontractors numbering over 100; some 8 firms of architect-engineers; representatives of the designers of the plant, the Carbide & Carbon Chemicals Company; and the employees of these various organizations, totaling some 20,000 people.

As one might expect, relationships between and among so many groups, with so many widely divergent goals, are very complex. The construction people strive to get the plant built, the Commission to see that it is built on schedule and according to specifications, and the operating people to make certain that the plant will operate when it is built. And when one adds to these complications of relationship the overriding necessity for doing much of the construction work and all of the operating work in an atmosphere of security, one begins to appreciate the absolute requirement for delegation and control in order to avoid complete chaos. For us delegation and control have become a way of life.

Thus, not only have delegation and control within each organization become a must, but delegation and control between and among the many separate organizations on the plant site have been developed to a remarkable degree. To prevent complete disruption of effort by so many competing interests, it has been necessary to co-ordinate all activities, whether of constructional or operational nature, to the end that the forward thrust of plant completion might be maintained.

This has been accomplished on a project-wide basis by having all interagency planning arrangements made and all basic agreements stemming therefrom reached at the level of the tripartite general managership of the project — i.e., by the general manager of the Kiewit company, the area manager of the Commission, and the general manager of Goodyear. Each general manager then carries back to his line-of-command the understandings developed, and he delegates to the appropriate people the responsibility for carrying out his organization's part of the plan. In this way confusion arising out of the multiplicity of agreements and arrangements which might be made by numerous individuals at the various levels of supervision working across company lines with their opposite numbers in the other organizations — which very often is how we get things done in business — has been avoided.

This is all preliminary, perhaps, to the subject of delegation and control by the general manager, but the situation at the Portsmouth project does illustrate the absolute need for these techniques within an organization, particularly if it is to make an effective and positive contribution to any joint venture in which it finds itself.

No less important is the case for effective delegation and control within the organization that has no responsibility to any associated co-operating agencies, but is in the fortunate position of being able to determine its own policies and to set its own course. Most businesses are in this category.

This is certainly the day of the specialist, and it is a unique and unusually well-rounded general manager who can bring to bear on his judgments an intimate experience with the several specialties over which he has a nominal direction.

In our own case, at the Goodyear Atomic Corporation, there are production requirements, research and development problems, industrial relations difficulties, and the complications of purchasing and warehousing, engineering and maintenance, and financial planning and programing, all demanding and getting the attention of the particular specialist who is responsible, as division manager, for the effective conduct of his branch of the business. Because the normal degree of specialization is greatly sharpened by the particular nature of our task, it is well-nigh impossible for any one individual to have anything like complete and detailed knowledge within all the separate divisions of effort.

We early recognized that our work would proceed most effectively if the sum total of all the experience of the several specialists was brought to bear on the problems which regularly confront us and on the determination of policies which tend to develop a climate conducive to effective growth of the corporation and to efficient application of its efforts.

Accordingly, since our origin some two years ago, we have functioned through an operating committee arrangement wherein the seven division managers and the general manager make up an executive and administrative cabinet. Delegation with us is complete, with each division manager assuming responsibility for the efficient conduct of his particular phase of the operation.

As an example of how this delegation works in one area, consider the matter of security. Here our authority to classify material as top secret, secret, or confidential comes to us through a written delegation from the Atomic Energy Commission. Our redelegation of this authority follows echelons of supervision within the corporation, with all delegation made in writing and its scope clearly stated.

Similarly, in other areas of operation the Commission provides for us, and requires of us, clear lines of delegation of authority to the end that those invested with authority, and only those, may enter into agreements and make commitments. For example:

> When we communicate with the Atomic Energy Commission about any particular phase of our activities — and this is many times daily — all letters are prepared for the general manager's signature by the division manager in whose realm of responsibility the subject matter lies. If the item is one entailing a high degree of specialized knowledge, the division manager may, in turn, delegate to one of his specialists the assignment of preparing the letter.
>
> Similarly all correspondence coming from the Commission is signed by its area manager and is directed to the general manager of the Goodyear Atomic Corporation, whence it then fans out through delegation to the division managers and their staffs.

Now the routing of all communications through the general manager does not mean that he studies every letter in great detail or attempts immediately to render a decision with respect to a particular problem. But he is responsible for delegating the problem at once and seeing that a particular individual responds to the Commission with alacrity.

The point is that we must know what is going on. To be specific, suppose there is a problem involving engineering activity. If an engineering division superintendent crosses company lines and corresponds directly with his opposite number in the Commission, then neither the Goodyear general manager nor the AEC area manager knows about it. But by having communications come to the general manager, he is provided with the knowledge that the Commission has raised a question which calls for a quick answer. Moreover, he knows that he has given the engineering division manager this question to handle, and he has an opportunity for checking soon to see that the Commission gets a satisfactory answer by the time it is wanted.

There is in our operation a factor which is not usually present in strictly private business, that is, the flow into our offices of bulletins, guides, and program changes originated by the Atomic Energy Commission and sent to us for informational purposes. Some of this material is directive in nature and some is permissive. But whether this AEC material is directive or whether it is permissive, it all falls within the purview of our contractual obligations, and it is essential that good lines of communication exist to speed these matters on their way. For example:

If the security classification of a certain phase of our work has been changed by Commission ruling — and this happens frequently in classification procedures — it is of extreme importance to get that information to the people working in the area affected, to the end that if stricter security is called for, it may be applied at once; or, conversely, if a declassification has occurred, costly effort to safeguard the downgraded matter may be discontinued.

We have found that our operating committee system of management control gives us the channels of rapid dissemination of information required in our business. This comes about through the fact that the division manager involved has participated in the discussion of the particular matter at hand. He, in turn, meets with his superintendents to explain the decisions reached by the operating committee. Because he has been a party to the decision, because the decision has developed out of the contribution of several individuals in the free give-and-take of a committee meeting, we find that an acceptance is gained and a disposition to co-operate is obtained greatly in excess of that which comes about as a result of arbitrary, one-man decision.

It is certainly pertinent to point out here that, because of his unique interests and abilities, the approach of the specialist to his problems is that of the analyst, while the approach of the generalist is that of the synthesist. In any business there are situations where each specialist — the production manager, the personnel director, the research director, the sales manager — feels and often acts as if his area of concern were the most important, the one without which the enterprise would falter.

It is here that the generalist — in our discussion, the general manager — must assume the role cut out for him. Out of the often conflicting needs of the several specialists, out of their importunities and representations, he must synthesize a solution to the problem which is creative, constructive, and at the same time acceptable.

To the extent that this synthesis is brought about in a climate of mutual understanding, of full participation, and of active co-operation — to that extent will the full potential of the management team be released. For what we are thinking about when we speak of effective delegation and control is not so much an arbitrary technique as it is a matter of *esprit de corps,* the ready and willing assumption of responsibility by those to whom authority has been delegated. This is accomplished only under conditions that are conducive to the free interplay of ideas, experience, and judgment.

In a Retail Store Holding Company

*By W. Earl McCormick**

The subject of effective delegation and control by the general manager is intriguing to me because I believe most companies enjoy

* Mr. McCormick is Vice President and Director, Allied Stores Corporation. He has been in the merchandising field since 1929, first with the Hahn Department

success to the degree that the general manager in fact exercises effective delegation and control. This may even transcend in importance the competitive position of the company's products or services. While effective delegation is important for a small, closely knit organization with perhaps but one plant, it becomes a *must* for a company with far-flung operations. This is especially true if the end products or services of each unit are to be tailored for marketing within the local trading area of the unit.

It seems to me the achievement of effective delegation and control for single-unit or multiple-unit operations — will be dependent on many factors, among which the following five will usually be found:

1. The establishment of a principal aim or objective.
2. Creation of the form of organization designed to achieve the principal aim.
3. Clear definition of the areas of responsibility.
4. Delegation of these areas of responsibility to qualified executives.
5. Effective administration and control.

Since the first three — establishment of the principal aim or objective, creation of the form of organization designed to achieve the principal aim, and clear definition of the areas of responsibility — are primarily concerned with purpose and form, they might well be classified as the science of delegation. The last two — selection of qualified executives for each area of responsibility and effective administration — could well be called the art of delegation and control, because the human element is dominant in these factors.

As an interesting illustration substantiating the importance of these five factors, let me describe the experience of the Hahn Department Stores Corporation when it was a newly formed holding company some 25 years ago. The example used is in no way a criticism of the company management because the usual problems of adjustment were further aggravated by depressing external influences in the period 1929 to 1933, which some readers may remember.

Stores Corporation; and then with its successor company, the Allied Stores Corporation. In his present position, he supervises the operations of a group of stores in Michigan and Ohio.

The company, which brought 27 formerly independent department stores into the fold, announced its principal aim in these words:

"To retain most, if not all of the advantages of the individual, locally owned department store and to obtain most of the advantages of the chain-store operation."

In most instances the former presidents and owners of the stores remained on the job as general managers of their respective units. Prior to the sale of his store, each local president had made all the required decisions with the advice and consent of his own board of directors. After the sale, it was necessary for the holding company to define those areas of responsibility which were reserved for the chief executive and his staff in the central office and those areas resting with the general manager of each unit. A basic problem, stated in the vernacular, was: Who had the ball? Was it with the general manager of each unit, or had it passed to the central office?

Of course, to some former owners, now local general managers, surrendering any part of their previous complete responsibility, or even some prerogatives, was extremely distasteful; but, more important, to many such an approach was considered most unsound. The newly organized central staff had some bitter lessons to learn, in spite of its many helpful contributions.

The present chief executive of Allied Stores (Hahn Stores' successor), when he assumed his responsibilities 20 years ago, reexamined the principal aim of the holding company and found it sound. But he took the next essential step and determined that the organization form, as well as definition of areas of responsibility, should be dedicated to the achievement of that purpose. With the announcement and implementation of this basic concept, the solution of the problems began to emerge, namely, that each store organization should be complete and self-contained, and that services from the central office should be of a character to supplement and intensify these self-contained store organizations. It seems rather clear cut — and I can verify this from experience — that with the announcement and implementation of that simple statement, everybody who had a responsibility knew exactly what it was and could go to work.

Today in Allied, the general manager of a store recognizes that he has the full responsibility for its operation. He has as supplemental aids to himself and his staff the assistance of a group of specialists in the headquarters of the company. He also has the advantages that come from co-operation and exchange of ideas and information with 72 other stores. On his board of directors is a vice president of the parent company who, because of his experience and familiarity with the many problems of the member stores, is able to lend helpful guidance. The general manager is the chief executive of the local unit and in fact one of the chief officers of the parent company.

In line with this philosophy, the delegation to market representatives, such as the central-office or field buyers, is always made by the store people. The store executives have the responsibility for any merchandise that comes to their store. They, in turn, may delegate to their counterparts in the marketing division of Allied the authority to go and do thus and so for them. Once they delegate, the store people obviously have to accept the end result of what a particular market representative does for them; however, the amount of delegation given by the store manager is in keeping with the previous performance of that market representative.

Of course, if the stores do not utilize to any degree the services of a market representative who is out in the field buying, it obviously expresses a lack of confidence; and then we have to look into the causes of this lack of confidence. These may be revealed when the store buyers have the opportunity annually of rating their counterparts in the central office.

There is no problem of separating responsibility of line and staff personnel. The final responsibility rests in the store because the store has the privilege of declaring what it wants and what it will accept.

All this is necessary, it seems to us, if we are to retain most, if not all, of the advantages of the individual, locally owned department store and, at the same time, to obtain most of the advantages of a chain operation.

So far in this discussion we have been concerned with the form or science of effective delegation and control. Effectual working with and through the human element may be construed as the art of this subject. Form is important as a guide, but performance is dependent on people. In fact, an able general manager must recognize that even though he establishes a perfect pattern of organization on paper, it will be necessary to temper that form in order to meet the capacities of the people selected. While this need obviously means compromise with perfection, the only sin in such a course could be the failure of the general manager to know of the compromise and also the extent to which it is carried. He cannot or should not compromise with inherent ability.

Since the general manager is truly the key person in the art of securing effective delegation, it is necessary that he have a great combination of qualities. What he does or what he can do is dependent on his capabilities in working with those responsible to him. His qualifications, therefore, are worthy of some attention. I believe that to have effective delegation and control you have to have an effective person at the top. Therefore, I choose to devote more attention to this particular phase of our science.

Along with good character and the degree of physical fitness required, the general manager should have at least the following attributes:

1. *The ability to evaluate the capacity of people for executive responsibility.* Such an important requirement hardly needs elaboration. The general manager has had the opportunity of watching people grow at various stages in the organization. They have been assigned different tasks, and he has observed the results. Accordingly, he should be able to determine an individual's general capacity for assignment to management responsibility.

2. *The skill of a good administrator.* A prime requisite under this qualification is the ability of the general manager to organize his *own* job. This may sound trite, but there are more than a few

examples of companies whose success is limited or even denied because the general manager lacks this qualification. Obviously in such instances the general manager not only impedes the work of those responsible to him, but also sets a very bad example. I have observed, and I am sure you have, persons charged with top responsibility who are so busy they do not have time to work with the people who report to them. Subordinates who cannot get to the general manager may line up outside his office and waste their time and effort, all because the boss is unable to organize his own time and his own job.

3. *The recognition that his responsibilities, rather than his prerogatives, are the matters of prime consideration.* Is he a leader? Or is he a boss, who wears that badge on his sleeve? I think we have all observed the general manager who seeks to rise and has done so, but who forgets that performance is what enabled him to get where he is. He assumes the boss has prerogatives that are not of less importance than his responsibilities. It is unfortunate when he allows himself to be so deceived. Subordinates promptly come to know the true facts and govern their actions accordingly.

4. *A willingness to delegate and to place responsibility for performance, together with the requisite authority for execution of assignments.* If executives junior to the general manager are to produce and to grow, they must be given proper responsibilities and the necessary power to fulfill such responsibilities. This starts with a willingness to delegate and place responsibility on others. I am sure we have all observed the general manager who lacks this qualification. Consequently, he limits the development of people and, therefore, the development of the company, the two being closely knit together.

5. *Acknowledgment of the good performance of others.* Due recognition for a superior job is the responsibility of the general manager and the right of the one who performed it. (On the other hand, avoidable failure deserves proper criticism.) I think in growing up we have all known people who participate in a job but feel that no others should share in the credit for the production.

One questions whether or not people who claim all the credit are entirely responsible for their deeds.

6. *The courage to make decisions, acting on facts and not on emotions.* The responsibility for making decisions is great even with all the facts at hand. Avoidable delay can be harmful to the morale of the organization. Decisions too often based on emotion may lead executives responsible for making recommendations to tailor them accordingly. The general manager cannot procrastinate and thereby hold up people responsible to him in their tasks.

7. *Imagination.* It is the general manager's responsibility to look ahead as well as to handle the current operations. He must encourage his team to grow and to take advantage of opportunities still to be had.

8. *The respect of his associates.* This qualification is not based on the position occupied by the general manager; instead it is based on the contribution he makes to the success of those with whom he works. This is an attribute he must earn. I believe few can succeed without the genuine respect of others. Particularly that is true in our business associations. When we think of our superiors, we ask, "What do they contribute to us to make us better in our jobs?" That does not mean they must know our particular specialties as well as we are supposed to know them, but certainly from experience they can observe us and help us avoid errors.

I have always found that it is the obligation and purpose of the general manager to aid another in the performance of his particular responsibility. He must guide and counsel his associates that they may be able to do a superior job.

9. *Ability to be a good team leader.* The general manager's success — or failure — is dependent on his associates. It is his obligation to elicit ideas, no matter how conflicting they may be, from all his people. It is also his job to be able to resolve conflicting ideas into a common goal which can and will be accepted by all. It is the goal of the company to which everyone is dedicated, but the general manager has the duty to hear conflicting opinions of his people, and it is their obligation to give their opinions to him. But once the course has been decided, all must pursue the common goal.

10. ***The will to succeed, which in turn must be inculcated in each member of the executive team.*** I think that quality needs no further emphasis. The will to succeed—the will to do—has to start at the top with the chief executive.

In the selection of general managers of member stores of our company, these qualities are among the important ones that we look for. Some, of course, can be acquired, but not all of them.

Real stress is constantly placed on the need for good administration by these general managers. They need and have a lot of help. One of the pitfalls is the belief that, to have a job done well, the manager must do it himself. That type of person is due for a short career as a general manager because of the limited number of matters he can handle personally. More important than the consequences to himself, however, would be the effect on the organization of the general manager's failure to lead, teach, and direct those to whom execution is the prime job. He must add to the quality and quantity of work produced by those responsible to him. He has the job of making those people better executives than they would be without him.

The general manager must establish standards of performance for each operation that are clearly understood and accepted by those responsible for execution. He has the personal obligation of knowing exactly how well his subordinates are carrying out their responsibility. The amount of information needed, its use, and the manner of obtaining it will vary among companies. In retailing, most stores have monthly budgets for planned sales and expense. If these budgets have been made realistically, performance reports showing "actual" and "plan" quickly reflect the strengths and the weaknesses of the operations of the stores.

There are many ways for a general manager to appraise the status of his organization. There are division reports which each store manager receives, and copies of which are usually sent to the parent company. But the general manager is not required to peruse each report in detail. He usually has an assistant, maybe two, who can, after proper instruction, review those reports for areas of strength or weakness. Without a great deal of routine checking, the general manager can know quickly at least where there are areas of weakness.

I have also found it helpful for a general manager to follow the principle of spot checking. He may not look at all reports that come in, but he should on occasion make a spot check of them. From the report of a division he can pretty fairly judge its relative status in a few moments; and as he goes through a store the general manager can again do a spot-checking job. While it is not his responsibility to perform every function of the store, he must know that all of them are being carried out. It takes but a couple of minutes to find out what is going on. For example:

Very recently in visiting one of our stores, I asked the general manager if *X* function had been carried out. He replied, "You know, I just didn't have time to check on it." So while we were in a particular department, I said, "Let's go to the office and get the record." I know we spent only about 10 minutes on it; I made a note of the time for two reasons. Not only did we find part of the answer to our problem, but also I was able to demonstrate the relatively short time it took to verify whether operations were being carried out. It was my job to demonstrate to the general manager that checking on an operation could be done, and I think he now knows that it can be.

In Allied, the parent company executives discuss plans with the general managers of the member stores—at least twice a year, on planned sales and expense. Local conditions play a dominant role in these plans. There must be agreement between the general manager and the company officer reviewing the store plans. Later, in checking performance against plan, the chief effort is devoted to guidance and stimulation rather than to control. *Control as an end in itself can be a hindrance to productive effort.*

In all of this discussion, it has been evident that the human element is paramount. The general manager must realize that one of his obligations is to bring along others who will be qualified to succeed him. He cannot forget that his tenure of office is relatively limited, even if he is a young man. The general manager who recognizes his obligation to bring along others will not only delegate important segments of the business to subordinates but will also do his best to provide guidance and counsel. He will demand performance as a practical matter and because in itself it is good training. Effective delegation requires a person of stature since only such a person is willing and anxious to have others grow. Sometimes people who aspire to and eventually achieve the role of general manager overlook similar aspirations on the part of those struggling to climb.

To men coming up the ladder, opportunity to perform should be uppermost. Some who seek both opportunity and ultimate reward at the same time may be more interested in the badge than in demonstrating capability. Executives at all levels will know of the general manager's willingness to provide opportunity. If this condition prevails, they will be anxious to perform well in their present capacity. Good performance will then earn the right to consideration for further opportunity.

The general manager must remember that he and also his subordinates are human. Neither he nor they are functional machines. The recognition of people as he moves through the store or plant is highly important. It is not difficult in walking through a store or plant with the general manager to tell by the manner of the greeting whether "Hello, John" or "Good morning, Mabel" is the usual custom. The recognition of people is helpful in good production. Furthermore, it is the general manager's obligation to counsel not only with his immediate subordinates but also with those junior to them regarding their progress and ambition. The open-door policy should exist in fact.

A considerable portion of this discussion has been devoted to stressing the importance of the role of the general manager in securing effective delegation and control. I hold the conviction that to the extent that he is an able, inspiring leader, he will create and develop a top executive team whose performance under his guidance will earn an enviable record for the company.

In a Medium-Size Bank

*By William B. Walker**

In discussing the topic under consideration, it is almost axiomatic to say that in any well-run business organization not only must there be the proper kind of delegation of authority but also control. Those two words are, of course, significant; however, the most important in this topic is the word "effective." To arrive at a situation in which you have the most effective control and delegation, I believe there are four factors which must be taken into consideration. First, the size of the organization; second, the nature of the business; third, the objectives of the business; fourth, the morale of the organization.

In presenting a few observations on this topic, I am going to use the case method of approach. I will try to outline for you the development that has taken place in our own institution over a period of some 25 years; and will attempt to show you how a change of atmosphere and philosophy, based on the impact of the four factors mentioned above, have given a far better measure of effective delegation and control, even though I am sure there are considerably more improvements in the techniques which can be made.

First, as to size. In March of this year, our bank showed total resources of more than $200 million. We have approximately 500 employees, including 33 officers. Our bank ranks about 116th in size out of a total of some 12,000 banks. It is fair to state that an institution of this size in this industry is considered a medium-size business. With our size and with three locations in the central part of the city, not only are our officers afforded an opportunity to be in almost daily communication with each other, but also with a large majority of the employees. This, of course, is in sharp contrast to

* Mr. Walker is President of the First National Bank of Philadelphia. Becoming associated with this bank in 1928, he progressed through its lending operations and assumed the presidency about four years ago.

the extremely large financial institutions with a greater number of employees and officers and with scattered branches; and, therefore, our approach to effective delegation and control, in all probability, is quite different in that we undoubtedly have more leeway.

Second, as to the nature of our business. We are a commercial bank with the usual operating, investment, loan, and trust departments. While, of course, we are a depository for our customers' funds and we lend money, on the whole it can be said that our product has no dimensions or specific form. We are a service institution and the product we sell is "service and brains." It is an interesting fact—and an important one—that of the total number of people on the bank's payroll, probably one-half or more are in almost daily contact with the customers who provide us with our business. Authority in varying degrees must be delegated to accomplish our objectives.

Third, as to our objectives. In other words, what are we out to accomplish? Our goals are no different from those of any other business. We do have one unique feature and that is our primary objective to protect the funds entrusted to us by our depositors. With this always in mind, we can then state that our goals are no different from any others. We are out to make a reasonable amount of money for our stockholders. We are an economic unit in the private enterprise system, and our stockholders are entitled to, and should receive, a fair return on their investment. Carrying on beyond these objectives, we want our people to be responsible citizens in the community, and we encourage officers and employees to have outside community activities. We are anxious to pay our people good salaries. We want to provide interesting and challenging work for those who can measure up to it. And we want our employees to have a sense of belonging to the organization.

As far as a case study is concerned with regard to our own organization, it has been interesting to me to look back over the past 25 years and observe the changes that have taken place in our bank. For the past 12 or 13 years, there has been a vigorous program of development. The bank has shown substantial but, at the same time, sound growth; and I firmly believe that this has been accomplished to a large degree by establishing delegation of authority and control and by making it effective.

There was a time when there was no real concerted effort to carry out any stated or known objectives; various functions and, in particular, many individual efforts were carried on in a more or less independent and loose manner. It is probably true that some heads of departments knew more about the policies of the bank than many of the officers. Department heads frequently had meetings, but the officer group had never had a regular program of meetings to discuss the bank's activities. There was no program for the development of potential leaders; and, therefore, there was no conscious thought given to the recruitment of new, able personnel. Certain accounts in the bank were in reality the property of an individual officer rather than the bank itself. The bank did grow, of course, during those years in spite of this lack of co-ordination. From the standpoint of protection to the depositors, I have no doubt that that function was being adequately cared for.

Within the past 12 or 13 years, however, there has been a complete shift in philosophy. Recognizing the need to delegate certain authorities in order to accomplish stated and known objectives, a number of steps have been taken. Because so many of the staff deal directly with our customers, the staff had to be organized in such a manner that it could operate as a team, and I use that word "team" advisedly, even though I know it sounds trite.

First of all, the officers are brought together as a group, and they meet frequently at regular intervals. All matters pertaining to the bank's activities are discussed fully and frankly. Before an officer can effectively and properly carry out his duties, we think he should be thoroughly informed about every possible phase of our activities because there are so many cross-currents and interrelated factors involving a customer's business with its bank. The meetings are not limited to any prearranged agenda. Senior officers comment on their particular functions, and the younger officers are encouraged to ask questions and discuss any matter about the bank that comes to their minds. One meeting usually is devoted exclusively to a thorough explanation of all the items appearing on our detailed operating statement and balance sheet. Probably there is no financial statement that can conceal as much as the bank statements usually seen in publications. We think that all the men should know what goes into the make-up of our financial statements, and it is most revealing to hear the questions asked by many of our younger officers.

We believe that a customer is really a customer of the bank and not a customer of any particular individual. At the same time, while one particular individual may take the lead in servicing a customer, we try to see that there are others who are fully familiar with the ramifications of the account and that our customer knows it. This works two ways. It not only prevents a void in the event a particular officer is absent, but, at the same time, gives an opportunity for others — particularly younger men — to have a sense of belonging. And a sense of belonging can be brought about more effectively if there is a real delegation of authority.

Secondly, the bank embarked a few years ago on a definite program for recruitment of able, new personnel. These men have been brought in with the distinct understanding that if they measure up to our qualifications, both as to intelligence and to ability to get along with the rest of the organization, responsibility will be passed along to them as fast as they can take it. In this connection, I was intrigued by an expression used by Dean Stanley Teele. He spoke about "selling short"; that is, purposely giving a man responsibility sometimes before he has actually demonstrated ability to perform, in the hope that he shows that he deserves it after it has been given to him. In this sense, we have done just that on occasions in our bank. It may be that we have had to relax somewhat the amount of control but, at the same time, our experience in this regard has proved most satisfactory.

We do remind ourselves from time to time that we should not be overoptimistic in giving untried men challenging opportunities because we recognize there is the danger of overdelegation of responsibility leading to a weakening of managerial authority. This is, however, a risk we think we should assume but, at the same time, safeguard against it.

Because of our size and the nature of our organization, we believe that we are on the right course to accomplish a number of our objectives although we consider that we are on a "shakedown cruise." We are not adhering strictly to the finely drawn, formal organizational chart, but management has subscribed wholeheartedly to the theory of delegation and has been learning how to apply it to our own particular situation. We are trying on this "shakedown cruise" to set up our organization around the men we have. During the early stages of a program of this kind, it is necessary to take into consideration the people you already have, their skills and capabilities, and what you can do with them. We expect as we go along that our informal organization for delegation and control will evolve into one that is more scientific. We will need this, in due course, as we bring in new people.

We feel that it is the size of the organization, the nature of the operations, and the objectives which will affect the specific means of accomplishing effective delegation and control. Experience has taught us that the right climate is the prime requisite and that progress can be made even by somewhat unscientific and informal means.

In a Textile Machinery Company

*By David F. Edwards**

As the oldest contributor to this chapter, perhaps I am entitled to the privilege, usually accorded the elderly, of indulging in a bit of reminiscence. And perhaps this will serve a useful purpose, for what I am about to refer to points up a significant contrast between a very large corporation and the smaller organization with which I have been associated all the latter part of my life.

In 1911, three years before the outbreak of World War I, I was given a very minor and inconsequential job with General Motors

* Mr. Edwards is Chairman of the Board, Saco-Lowell Shops. His section is presented here although because of illness it was not possible for him to participate in the panel session on which this chapter is based. Portions of Mr. Edwards' prepared paper were read to the audience.

Company. General Motors had been put together in 1908 by William C. Durant, and three years later it was still simply a collection of completely separate plants operating in much the same way as they had been before the consolidation. Some plants were well managed and some were not. But each one went its own way to a large extent.

When I began my job, the general offices were over O'Brien's grocery store on Woodward Avenue, opposite the old and now defunct Pontchartrain Hotel, around the bar of which a new motor car company was organized about once a month, or so the saying went in Detroit at that time. The federal income tax was not yet in existence. Labor unions were still weak and of little influence on management. Industrial engineering, as a profession and as an important factor in management, was just beginning to emerge. It was indeed a period of very rugged individualism, and the climate was not favorable to many aspects of modern management as we know it today.

In 1910 a group of bankers had undertaken to refinance General Motors with an issue of $15 million five-year gold notes, and during the five years the notes ran the banks had virtual control of the property. They were disturbed, and not without reason, over the go-as-you-please fashion in which each of the subsidiary plants was operating. And having little interest in — and even less knowledge of — human behavior in business organizations and the way in which men react to controls, they decided to set up a central production control authority in the Detroit office.

I recall the man who was brought on from the East to head up this new department. He was a lamb led to the slaughter. He had to deal with men like Charles Nash, later founder of the Nash Motors Company, and Walter Chrysler, later founder of the Chrysler Company, who were among the able, tough-minded, two-fisted managers operating in the different subsidiary plants. I watched the experiment, for the two years it lasted, with skepticism as to its success and with growing sympathy for the man who headed it up.

Of course, the central authority broke down, and I never forgot the lesson it taught, even in that period of primitive management concepts and methods. The lesson was that a very large measure of decentralization with respect to operating responsibility and authority is essential for the successful operation of a group of subsidiary or branch plants. And the stronger and abler and more valuable the men are who run these plants, in all likelihood the more difficult they are to control and the more they resent central-office interference at the local plant level.

Delegation and control mean different things to different men. If the general manager has the kind of temperament that makes him inclined to be suspicious of other men, if he lacks inner certainty in the soundness of his judgment in choosing and placing men, if he has something of the martinet in him and enjoys the exercise of power for its own sake, he is not likely to do a wholehearted job of delegating. Nor will his subordinates have the freedom of action that will enable them to do their best work, develop their powers and aptitudes, and grow in managerial capacity. For example:

> I recall a factory executive who seemed to delight in calling his group together at rather frequent intervals and lecturing them on the importance of being "self-starters" in their jobs, of being men of initiative and independent judgment who did their own thinking, made their own decisions, and carried them out with competence and dispatch. But having said all this, he would then keep them under a kind of malicious observation in a rather sly way, looking for mistakes that he could needle them with rather than giving them constructive help in learning how to avoid making mistakes in the future.

The case of this man illustrates the point that mere delegation by the general manager is not enough. The old idea that the way to train a manager is to throw him into the job and let him sink or swim is rather generally discredited today. Delegation of authority is only the first step. After delegation, the attitude of the general manager; the way he uses the routine accounting controls, budget figures, performance standards, and means of communication; the kind of personal relationships he creates among his subordinates; and his own relationship with them—all these factors determine how effectively the general manager does his job by working through his subordinates to get things done.

Moreover, he cannot give authority with one hand and take it away with the other. Unless the key men in the organization have confidence in one another as a team and in the general manager as an understanding boss whose experience and judgment are available to them when they need help — available in a way that makes them know they are welcome to ask for help — then the delegation of authority does not adequately accomplish its purpose.

Let me comment at this point on the overworked phrase "staff and line organization." Of course there must always be men in the organization — some of them specialists and technicians — who have time to think and plan, to assemble facts and analyze them, and to make recommendations. But why make a point, at least in a moderate-size organization, of labeling them staff men as distinguished from line men? Not infrequently that labels them as a class set apart from the toil and grime of the day's operations, and builds up a kind of hostility toward them on the part of the men who are hard-pressed to get their daily chores done on schedule.

I prefer to think that all men in the organization should try to think clearly about their jobs, work hard at them, maintain good relations with their fellows, and get the results expected of them, whether the results be the fabrication of so many units of product per day, or the effective handling of a problem of labor relations, or the improvement of the product through research, or the provision of useful accounting figures for the control and guidance of the business as a whole. Each one's contribution to the over-all effectiveness of the organization can be just as important as another's, regardless of whether his job is classified as line or staff — provided always that the general manager has not indulged himself too freely in fringe personnel and expanded his overhead beyond sound limits.

And that brings me to the question of the size of an organization as a factor in determining how delegation and controls shall be handled by the general manager. I have read some of the articles and addresses by Ralph Cordiner, president of General Electric, about the way that huge company has decentralized its management and delegated responsibility and authority to the organization units at the operating level. Mr. Cordiner's problem, of course, calls for a wholly different kind of handling than does, for example, the problem in my own business — the Saco-Lowell Shops — which employs up to 7,000 men in periods of good volume.

In a business of our size it is possible for the chief executive to know all the key men in his organization. He can see them often enough to be able to evaluate with some degree of accuracy both their current performance and their future potential. He does not have to have the same kind of elaborate reports on operating results or personnel, or the same kind of highly developed staff or service groups as are found necessary in a big organization. His management can be more personalized, less aloof and detached — a management that relies more on human relationships than on reports and charts, though there should be enough of the latter to provide a sound factual basis for reaching well-founded conclusions and decisions.

What I am trying to say is that in an organization employing less than 10,000 people, for example, there is still room and opportunity, and perhaps need, for more of the kind of personalized management that prevailed a generation ago. Call it old-fashioned, if you like, by today's criteria, but it had its merits. Something goes out of management when a business becomes so big that the general manager becomes a name and a title rather than a personality to all but a handful of his subordinates. And because of that it is necessary to delegate and control to an increasing degree.

Let me add, however, that in spite of the difficulties created by the growth of an organization beyond a certain size, there are also in many areas of industry great compensating advantages which have enabled big business to make incredible advances in increasing productivity and lowering costs.

Let me close my section with one final statement that goes against the current of the stream of management thinking today. We hear a lot about the importance of the management team and the role of the general manager as the captain rather than the dominating personality. I have already paid my tribute to the importance of creating such a team. But I am not one of those who think that the team should be completely frictionless, that its operation should be so smooth, so free from emotional vibration, so slick in the way it functions, as to appear to be almost effortless. There is danger that such a team may become superficial and routine in the way it does its job.

In any business that is growing and moving forward there must be constant change, some of it painful, most of it controversial. And the gears of the management team will certainly clash and grind at times if the team is composed of strong, able, self-confident men, some of them preferably with a touch of genius and perhaps a little unpredictable in their actions. To keep such a team functioning well in spite of occasional, inevitable clashes is the one responsibility of the general manager that he cannot delegate.

Questions about Delegation

*An Open Discussion**

From the floor: Most of us are under the assumption that when you delegate responsibility to a subordinate, you let him take it and judge him afterwards. This is very difficult for a superior to do.

This leads to the question: *How do you judge acceptance of responsibility by the subordinate, and how do you get the superior to let go?*

Mr. Gracia: I was fortunate to work under an executive who was a good coach. I would find in my basket in the morning letters which I knew had been over his desk and which would have penciled notes on them telling me to do this or that or to go ahead and handle it as I thought best. And in the case of problems that I brought back to him with my recommendations, I subsequently learned his method of handling them and whether I was right or wrong, because, as a good coach, he took occasion to let me know

* Businessmen present at the panel session on which this chapter is based raised certain questions which brought about the interplay of ideas reported more or less verbatim in this section.

what action he had taken and what the outcome of each problem was. This executive was able to let go because he had a desire to check the ability of a subordinate, which is necessary for effective delegation. He was using delegation as a measure of acceptance of responsibility.

Mr. Walker: I likewise had good coaching as to the delegation of responsibility. There is another factor in my particular case. Having come up through the credit department, I think that nothing would stifle the personnel of the credit and loan departments more than my being called on to make all the decisions with regard to credits. I take the position that loan requests should be channeled through the credit department and the credit officers who have the responsibility for making proper investigations and subsequent recommendations.

I do not think you can draw a blueprint as to how you judge a person's acceptance of responsibility. It is just a matter of seeing who gets things done. Some people carry out assignments independently, competently, and fast, while others just do not measure up.

Mr. McCormick: First of all, would you delegate authority to anyone who has not shown evidence of some capacity?

Secondly, I would question delegation of authority to anyone who did not accept responsibility. There are many people in the world who will do a good job but do not care for responsibility. If they have not reached for responsibility, it is rather doubtful if you can successfully sell it to them.

As to letting go, I think that comes by degrees. People who are growing in responsibility have to find out how to let go, and they have to be coached.

From the floor: Here is a general question that seems to me as tough as it is important: *What are the governing considerations on which a general manager might decide whether to replace an executive to whom control has been overdelegated or withdraw a part of his authority?*

Mr. McCormick: It would appear to me that the general manager would have to determine the cause or causes and the extent of the deficiencies. Are they repetitive? Has the individual in question exercised sound judgment and enjoyed a good performance record worth previous responsibilities?

Withdrawal of all or a part of an executive's responsibility and authority can be devastating to him and more costly to the company than replacement. Loss of face is a big hurdle to overcome.

Mr. Gracia: This *is* a tough problem. I think it depends on whether a young man is ready to step up and be given some degree of responsibility which he has not been used to. That happens sometimes, and it makes a difference in your approach. There is a tendency on the part of the general manager to delegate some authority and at the same time protect a subordinate. That seems to be the human thing to do.

Particularly in the case of young men, I think that responsibilities should be delegated to them rather as questions are posed to a participant in a quiz program. The master of ceremonies encourages him by saying, "You are now at $500 leading to the gateway to the bank." Then the participant answers the question incorrectly and is told, "You are now back to $300, but you have another chance." This moving ahead and moving back are all part of the coaching system, but the coaching does not have to be done openly. However, you cannot expect a person to assume responsibility in an area unless he is given the whole job.

Mr. Walker: It does happen that where authority has been overdelegated, we have had to take steps and relieve the situation. We have found that when someone shows up as weak in his job and is not following through properly with responsibility given to him, we have been able to shift the work around in such a way that eventually he is not responsible to the fullest extent as before with that authority.

From the floor: The problem of whether or not to delegate responsibility applies to youngsters in the buying game when we do not know if they are quite ready for full responsibility. We often give them the name of acting buyer for six months or a year, and we help them. We tell them, "We think you have the potential, but you are not entirely ready for the full responsibilities of a buyer." Usually we do not have to pull their authority back, because they gain confidence and competence as they go along. We stay with them and coach them, and they accept our help because they know they do not yet have full responsibility.

From the floor: It seems to me the major executive in a department or in a business has to accept full responsibility for whatever his assignment is, and in sharing that responsibility with others he does it at his own risk. Now, if he is expected to coach and to help subordinates take on more responsibility, he begins, perhaps ideally, by presenting them with a written job description — a first outline of a plan of what he hopes each one will become.

But if a business is to be successful, the chief executive cannot abdicate his responsibility. He may feel he can dole it out a little at a time, according to his judgment of the capacity of the person with whom he is dealing. It has been my experience that, try as I might, ambitious as I have been to help all the men around me take on their proper share of the responsibility which I was perfectly willing to delegate, each of these men is different. What you may ideally do with one individual, you can do only partially with another. How to cope with these differences is one of the most obviously difficult tasks management has. It becomes a measure of ability to teach, as has been pointed out many times.

The informal control that you use to determine how well responsibility is accepted and how fully the job assignment is undertaken is actually a matter of judgment. Our purpose in business is not to let a man feel he is in error but to help him to avoid errors which are avoidable.

From the floor: What must you do when responsibility has been accepted and only partially performed? What do you do with that individual — immediately replace him, chop his head off, or try to work out a scheme to deprive him of his responsibility without his knowing it? It has been my experience that the situation is not improved very much by your going out and hiring a person with a big reputation. You know how the present employee thinks, and you are infinitely better off by doing, as Mr. Gracia says, a coaching job, rearranging his work, as Mr. Walker says, so that he still feels that he has responsibility.

While I would not hesitate to withdraw responsibility, I think it should be done—if at all possible—by giving the man the assistance and coaching he needs but at the same time keeping him at the level at which he has been established.

I am in a new business which has grown to a considerable size, and I know we face this problem almost every week. Furthermore, we are going to have this problem for the next 10 years. But I have learned from my experience to stay with the person of my first choice; a change in general managers or heads of departments is dangerous and rarely works out.

Conclusion

*By John D. Glover**

As I have followed our general managers discussing effective delegation and control, it seems there are a number of ideas which are especially worthy of being underlined.

Mr. Gracia, as I understood him, among other things, remarked how the requirements for delegation and control arise inevitably in organizations. The need for delegation arises ultimately out of the complex nature of business. The problems and processes of modern business invariably involve matters of highly technical natures in many fields—financial, legal, and operational. It is well-nigh impossible for anyone to have a high degree of technical competence in more than one or two of those fields. Accordingly, there must be division of labor among enough people so that the necessary kinds and degrees of skill can be brought to bear on the problems of the organization.

Also implicit in Mr. Gracia's observations, as I understood them, was the thought that many businesses are sufficiently large that the jobs—quite apart from their technical content—are just so *numerous* that numbers of people must be engaged in handling them.

* Mr. Glover, who served as moderator of the panel session on which this chapter is based, is Professor of Business Administration, Harvard Business School.

There is just so much to do that the work *must* be divided up and parceled out among them, if it is to get done.

Then, Mr. Gracia moved on to the matter of control. The jobs, having been divided up, must be brought back together again. After all, these jobs are not just being undertaken as ends in themselves, but as parts of an over-all effort. They must be meshed and synchronized. As Mr. Gracia was using the word, this is where control comes in — as a necessary function to get a synthesis among the parts of the whole.

Mr. Gracia set forth his ideas in relation to an organization which is constructing a billion-dollar plant, with some 20,000 people involved. In contrast Mr. Walker has discussed an organization of some 500 people. But it takes no stretch of the imagination to see that the smaller company also requires many kinds of skills to perform many kinds of jobs. The process of delegation is the very essence of effective administration of an organization.

Tying in with Mr. Gracia's ideas — or at least so I thought — Mr. McCormick pointed out that it is a pitfall for an executive to think that in order to get a job done well he must do it personally. The jobs which need to be done are so many, and the number of items an executive can handle himself are so few, that delegation *must* take place if the executive is to keep on top of his job — or even, perhaps, to *keep* his job.

Mr. McCormick has indicated another factor which he thinks also makes for delegation. That is the need for adept local superintendence, particularly where individual stores have competitive situations peculiar to their market, climate, variation of seasonal trends, and so on. These problems must be solved by the executives out in the field, not in the central office in New York. So the process of delegation is a necessary counterpart to the process of getting things done in a way that makes sense relative to local, specific situations.

Then there was another idea of Mr. McCormick connected with this one which struck me; and the *way* Mr. McCormick put it struck me too. He said that not only would the executive who failed to give — to delegate — scope for action and responsibility end up with a short career, but "more important," says Mr. McCormick — and I was interested in those words "more important" — "would be his failure to teach, lead, and direct those to whom execution is the prime job."

If I follow Mr. McCormick correctly, he is saying that the executive's job not only involves getting the work of the present done in the here and now, but — "more important" — he also has the job of building the organization for the future. There is, by this way of looking at things, a twofold yardstick he has to measure up to in every action and in every concrete case: To get the work done today — which I guess we will all take for granted; and *also* to help the people in the organization grow, so that tomorrow's work and next year's work will get done even better, even quicker, and even more easily.

Mr. Walker has presented a sketch of an organization in which the process of delegation had not taken place. While the amount of delegation is obviously a matter of degree, there is a point where an organization becomes cumbersome, where nobody knows what is going on, where the chief executives withhold information from employees, where there are symptoms of slowly declining morale — employees leaving the organization, and so on — until the organization no longer has the capacity to do the day's work. And then he has shown what management can accomplish when it awakes to the situation and takes action.

One of the passages in Mr. Edwards' discussion that I thought was especially interesting was where he dealt with the personal, inner qualities which go along with delegation or nondelegation by an executive. Mr. Edwards was saying that if the general manager is inclined to be suspicious, or if he lacks confidence in his own ability to choose and place men, if he is a martinet and overly fond of power, he is not likely to do a wholehearted job of delegating.

Mr. Edwards also went on to say that under such a man subordinates will not have the freedom of action people need to do their best work. I guess we could tie that thought back to the ideas of

Mr. Gracia and Mr. McCormick—that the jobs are so many and so complex that they simply *must* be divided up and distributed among a number of people, trained people, specialized people.

Perhaps it would not be too much to say, or too broad an inference to draw from all these ideas that delegation is of the essence, a first step, an indispensable aspect of administration—no delegation, no organization, and no results. Delegation is essential in an organization which is thriving rather than slowing down year by year.

This leads me to make some additional comments on our topic which I would like to throw in the hopper along with those of Mr. Gracia, Mr. McCormick, Mr. Walker, and Mr. Edwards.

When we talk about administration, we are inclined to look at it from just one point of view at a time—usually from *our own point of view.* We tend to identify ourselves with what we might call the "heroes" of the dramas and ideas that unfold themselves before us. For instance, all of us contributing to this volume have been thinking of delegation primarily from the standpoint of those who are doing the delegating and controlling. We have not been thinking about how delegation and control appear to those on the *receiving* end.

While I would not suggest for a moment that we should not take the point of view we have, it might be useful if we could look at delegation and control from the receiving end as well, and at the same time.

The delegator, in delegating, is letting go of something for which he is responsible. In the process of delegation, he is placing his organization, indeed, his own career—maybe even his own life in some situations—at least to some extent in the hands of someone else. In the matters delegated, he, personally, has less scope for action. That is what delegation looks like to him. Control, on the other hand, is likely to look to him like getting matters back into his own hands. This is a means for reassuring himself that all is well and safe. Unless—and this I think was implicit in Mr. Edwards' comment—the delegator is a big man, and a self-confident, well-adjusted man, he is likely to view delegation with at least a twinge of misgiving and to look at control with something at least of a bit of fondness and relief. With controls in his hands, he can recapture scope for action by himself.

But to the man on the receiving end, these very same things look different. To him delegation will look like *more* scope for action. It means greater freedom to express himself, to use initiative, and to be responsible. Control, on the other hand, restricts this scope for action, it curtails at least somewhat his individual liberty or license.

When you look at it this way, I think it is easier to understand why it is that often between the man who does the delegating and the controlling, and the man who *receives* the delegation and who is controlled, there is a difference of opinion as to whether there is enough, too little, or too much delegation or control.

I do not mean at all to say that *conflict* is inherent between the two parties to this process. I think I have seen many cases where the people involved seem to have worked things out between them very well indeed. This seems to be especially the case when both have a very realistic view of the world in general and of themselves in particular.

But consider what the situation must become if the superior is overly timid, or has an undue opinion as to his own abilities — and where the subordinate is unduly ambitious and eager. They are likely, both of them, to be unhappy whatever arrangement they have as to delegation and control. The one will be in a perennial sweat lest he delegate too much or lose control, and the other will constantly chafe that he is hemmed in.

A reversal of these personal qualities between the two parties will not help matters much. A timid subordinate will be fearful of opportunity. Opportunity necessarily involves unpredictables and unknowns. Opportunity involves risk and hazard. Scope for action may well be frightening to people who are timid or have spent too much of their lives tied to someone else's apron strings. A timid, dependent man, paired up with a bold, dashing, impetuous, cavalier sort of a boss will be panic-stricken a good bit of the time. And the boss will be fretful and impatient — and likely to wonder when, if ever, the younger generation will learn to stand on their own feet.

The timid subordinate will seek for the comforting enclosures of tight controls. But the brash superior will have too many other interests — too many irons in the fire — to be checking up on *him* all the time.

This idea could be expanded at some length. But the point I should like to make is that whether we are in the role of delegator and controller, or delegat*ee* and controll*ee* — and most of us are really in *both* positions in our organizations, being the subordinate of somebody and the superior of someone else — it ought to be instructive to look as realistically as we can at these processes of delegation and control from the *other* standpoint. A realistic size-up of the situation — of the talents and characteristics of ourselves and our colleagues — may help us see somewhat better the jobs of education and growth that are before us.

In the particular circumstance, such a realistic size-up may indicate that we ourselves must learn to be less timid, or to help the other man to gain more courage. Maybe we both need more of a touch of self-confidence. Or maybe things will be more the other way around — maybe a little tempering is in order.

In any case, this is just one other way in which the processes of administration involve processes of education. And, as in other educational enterprises, I suspect that example and precept are likely to be the most effective educational techniques.

EFFECTIVE DELEGATION AND CONTROL BY THE MANUFACTURING EXECUTIVE

Introduction

*By Charles M. Williams**

Delegation of authority and executive control have won widespread recognition as key concepts of administration. But to many executives these remain little more than "buzz words" — vague concepts without practical meaning in their working context.

Readers of this book are not theorists, I presume, but rather operating executives interested in building for themselves a working philosophy of delegation and control. This is no easy job. Even such a master of administration as General Clay says (in Part I) that no one fully understands the art of delegation; and the term "communication" as applied to the administrative process is almost a new word. Fifteen years ago there was little mention of the term in connection with administration; yet it is under discussion here as one of three key aspects of administration.

"Control" and "controllership," the concept of the accounts as a measure of control rather than as a historical record of events, again about 15 years ago were only just beginning to appear in business school curricula and in the literature of business. The words with anything like the meaning they have today were not in our working vocabulary. It is no wonder we find some of these concepts still rather elusive, despite such elucidation as that in the first part of this book. Real understanding and mastery of delegation, communication, and control are, I think, the work of a lifetime.

While some of us may be impressed with the vagueness of these

* Mr. Williams, who served as moderator for the panel session on which this chapter is based, is Associate Professor of Business Administration, Harvard Business School.

concepts as we try to apply them, I had a somewhat contrary experience recently. During several months' stay in a Mediterranean country, I had the opportunity to observe the operations of the executives of some large business enterprises there. One dominant impression resulted. Despite all our difficulty in verbalizing our concepts of administration, particularly the concepts of delegation and control, by comparison we in this country have come a long way in our understanding and practical application of key concepts. One can appreciate then the progress we are making when he sees important business organizations in other countries where the concepts of administration that we take as basic, if imperfectly developed, are hardly known at all.

In this chapter three manufacturing executives — a president, a vice president, and a plant superintendent — will draw from their varied experience in presenting their ideas as to how the manufacturing executive can be effective in delegation and control in his operations.

From the President's Point of View

*By Edward J. Hanley**

I have no doubt that most readers have had called to their attention, at one time or another, the passage from chapter 16 of Exodus, verses 13–27, which bears directly on the subject under discussion in this book:

Jethro, father-in-law of Moses, came to Moses who was spending himself listening to the troubles and complaints of his people. Moses was working from dawn until dark, and his people were standing around in droves waiting to be heard. Jethro said to Moses, "The thing you do is not good."

He advised Moses to select able persons "from all Israel" and to organize his people into groups of thousands, hundreds, fifties, and tens,

* Mr. Hanley is President of Allegheny Ludlum Steel Corporation. Joining Allegheny as secretary in 1936, he subsequently was elected treasurer, vice president in charge of finances, executive vice president, and in 1951 president.

placing over each group one of these able persons. He suggested that Moses delegate authority to the leaders of these groups to deal with the people in most matters, passing on to Moses only the important issues.

This is a pretty good blueprint for a general plan of delegation of authority by a manufacturing executive. If the blueprint is followed successfully, there should not be many problems coming through to the top. In this connection, let me repeat the story of the man and wife who agreed on their wedding day that she would resolve all small questions and he would resolve all large ones. After many years, the husband stated that in his entire married life no large problems had arisen.

All members of the management team have to work within the confines of company policies. These policies are established by the board of directors, but they must be shaped largely by the president and his immediate staff, the other officers of the company. Generally speaking, company policies affecting the plants include the following:

1. General growth objectives.
2. Financial planning.
3. Operating policies.
4. Accounting policies.

The chief manufacturing executive and his organization have an important voice in determining these policies. Over-all objectives of a company are generally greatly influenced by what it is currently doing. Should the company do more of the same thing? Should it do other things? Should it stop doing some things it is now doing? Should it install new equipment or replace old equipment? Should it open a new plant or close an old one? Should it start manufacture of a new product line? A manufacturing executive does not have everything to say about such moves, but the opinion of the manufacturing organization might be determining in most of them.

Financial planning has to be tailored to suit over-all company objectives, though sometimes the situation might be reversed. Financial planning, in any event, may well control the rate of expenditure for new plant items. It may continuously affect inventory control.

And financial planning may have to be modified because of manufacturing exigencies.

Operating policies are the immediate concern of the manufacturing executive. It is important in multiplant operation that the fundamental ground rules be consistent. Whether or not employees involved are in the same labor union, general working conditions should be the same in each plant. Objectives with respect to quality, dealings between plant personnel and customers must be uniform within a company. In many cases, however, even operating policies cannot be determined without consultation with the sales and research organizations because, after all, the operating department is merely one arm of the body corporate.

Finally, since the results of all operations are ultimately recorded in the financial statements of the company, uniform accounting policies are essential so that all parts of the organization speak the same language. There must be a general understanding of these accounting policies and a general acceptance of the accounting plan —perhaps I should say respect for the accounting personnel. A manufacturing organization must have confidence in its accounting department because its financial progress is measured by the figures the accounting department produces.

So much for policy determination. Now what about carrying out the policies?

As an organization grows, it becomes absolutely necessary to delegate—again I refer the reader to the story of Moses and Jethro. Our problem becomes one of developing leaders so that they will exercise their authority wisely.

Delegation of authority is variously described; sometimes it is called decentralization, and I think this is a particularly descriptive term. There are, of course, varying degrees of decentralization. Many companies decentralize their bookkeeping and assume that they have decentralized their management. Some companies draw up an organization chart showing delegated responsibility but still retain a strangle hold from headquarters. Ordinarily there is not too much of a problem in decentralizing, at least to plant level. But some companies decentralize to the plant level only instead of insisting *as a company policy* that the plant manager, too, decentralize, delegating authority to the individual foreman in matters where the latter should have complete responsibility.

Assignment of authority, however, without a good means of measuring success or failure could be disastrous. Before a company decentralizes, therefore, over-all policies must be generally well understood. Further, good reporting practices in accounting are essential. If performance is not up to expectation, the manufacturing executive must recognize the situation immediately. If a superlative job is being done, he must be able to pat someone on the back at once.

To make all this more immediate, here is a brief outline of how we at Allegheny Ludlum try to make the broad program work:

We are organized with a plant manager as head of his plant. He reports to the vice president in charge of production, but he is responsible for the operation of his plant within the broad policy limits laid down for him by headquarters. We expect the plant manager to show results.

Headquarters is organized with a vice president in charge of production; a controller in charge of accounting; a director of industrial relations charged with over-all industrial relations problems, training programs, safety activities, and co-ordination of salary administration; a vice president in charge of sales; a treasurer watching over finances (including inventories); a vice president in charge of purchasing; a vice president in charge of research; and a vice president in charge of engineering. All functional personnel at the plants are responsible to their plant manager except in matters of policy. They are assisted in their jobs by their functional division heads at headquarters, whose responsibility is in matters of policy only. Frequent meetings are held of all works accountants, labor relations supervisors, training and safety administrators, to exchange ideas, help in co-ordination, and bring word to headquarters of policy problems which might require changes.

We have built up, over the past 17 or 18 years, reliable information concerning the relationship between profit and sales volume for our important product lines in each plant. We therefore have a measuring stick for progress in cost reduction in which all our men have great confidence. Our cost systems are well accepted by plant management. The acceptance is attained principally through having the right kind of accounting personnel; if they are competent and their work is good, they and their systems gain the necessary respect of operating personnel. In recent years we have installed much new cost-reducing equipment, and it is beginning to show results. We have also accelerated our incentive programs, all of which contribute to cost reduction. The combination of these things has encouraged interest in keeping costs down and has made our plant management extremely cost-conscious.

This interest in cost is not restricted to plant managers but is growing continuously throughout the manufacturing organization. There is an old saying, "Nothing succeeds like success." Changes that bring about cost reductions suggest other changes until the whole program becomes an enjoyable game — difficult but stimulating.

An interesting by-product of this program has been a speedup in financial statements until we are now in a position, without overtime, to have profit-and-loss results by the close of the fifth working day following the end of a month — three days earlier than previously. This enables those who have accomplished something in the month to get the lift that success always gives; at the same time it gives those who have not done so well a chance to improve in areas where they may not have appreciated that they were having trouble.

Emphasis on costs without corresponding emphasis on quality (reflecting the plant manager's obvious interest in production — quantity as opposed to quality) could have unfortunate results. We have laid down a fundamental company policy that *our quality will be second to none.* Our plant managers understand this thoroughly. In recent years we have developed within our plants a large organization of quality experts working for the plant manager in the plant metallurgical laboratory but having functional responsibility to the vice president in charge of research. If the operators depart from standard instructions in processing material, the metallurgical control man reports the departure first to the operating head of his department. If the situation is not corrected, he sends notification through his own functional superior in the plant to the plant manager. If the matter is still not resolved, the top quality-control man in the plant finally brings it to the attention of the vice president in charge of research, who then informs the vice president in charge of production. I do not know when such a situation has occurred. The duty of the plant metallurgical group is to help the plant manager maintain top quality, and the plant manager understands it.

With authority as far decentralized as it is at Allegheny Ludlum, one might wonder what the vice president in charge of production does. He advises with plant managers on their scheduling and operating plans; in many respects he serves as a conscience reminding them of things that might be overlooked. He co-ordinates production between plants where the same products can be made. He visits each plant two or three times each month to remind, to urge, to encourage, and only very occasionally to order. We have found that by delegating we build teamwork and enthusiasm which get the job done without commands. Plant managers meet at least monthly to discuss general plans and to help establish policies.

The functional heads operate in a similar manner. For example, the treasurer meets with the plant managers to discuss inventory control. They set objectives which fit in with his over-all plan and toward which the plant managers work. The controller meets with his works accountants at least once in three months to assure that accounting is co-ordinated and to discuss and resolve any policy problems. Under the controller there is an internal audit group which is continuously reviewing procedures at plants to make sure that practices are uniform. The group was organized in an attempt to see that details do not get out of control.

Generally speaking, we try continuously to impress on all functional personnel, both at headquarters and in the plants, that they are service people whose job it is to assist the line organization in carrying out its duties. The line is responsible for putting out the product, and the staff must accept its responsibility for serving the line.

There is another fundamental tenet which we continuously preach to the management organization: try to decentralize to the lowest rung on the supervisory ladder. We make every effort to resolve grievances at the foreman level. Not all of them can be resolved there, but a great many more are resolved there now than used to be when less effort was made. What we are after is participation in management from the foreman up. Our management participation programs, which operate under a training director in each plant, are primarily problem-raising, problem-solving conferences. We have other plans along these same lines—for example, a suggestion plan, which has been ready for installation for several months, and which we are holding until we feel that the management group all down the line is properly conditioned to make the plan a success.

For several years the industrial engineers have worked entirely through the foremen. At one time an incentive plan was established, the foremen were told about it, and at the same moment it was presented to the machine operators. More often than not the plan would be out of favor with the foremen. Now any incentive plan is presented first to the foremen—and, unless they are favorably disposed toward it, it is not presented to the operators at all.

Salary adminstration has recently been completely decentralized. Salary control is vested in the plant managers who operate within a sound salary plan which they have helped to develop. Under this plan they have a budget within which they must work, but they do not have to get any approval for a particular salary change.

We have tried hard recently to improve the morale of the management team. As vehicles to this improvement we have found two projects extremely helpful. We have bettered our housekeeping remarkably; and our people, both in the management group and in the working force, are now proud of their plants. This housekeeping drive has been as effective a morale builder as anything we have done. Three years ago our plants were dirty and untidy; today they are always ready for visitors. Incidentally, we find customers impressed when they visit clean plants.

The second morale-building project, growing partly out of the housekeeping program, is a concerted drive to improve the safety record. This, too, is a great morale builder not only among the management group but also among the workforce. We have one sizable plant in which there has been *no* lost-time accident for more than a six-month period. Every person in that plant is fully conscious of this record and is doing his best to see that it continues.

Quarterly, in the last two years, a group from headquarters has swung around the circle to visit each plant. The group has included the president, the executive vice president, the vice president in charge of production, his chief assistant, and the director of industrial relations. The trips have involved complete plant tours, usually a luncheon with the top supervisory group, and finally a meeting with the entire management team. We have taken the opportunity at these meetings to discuss important happenings, the preceding quarter's profit-and-loss results, the order picture, prospects for the near future, status of the plant program, safety record, and also the salary plan (which I mentioned earlier) as it was being developed. We have answered any questions to the best of our ability. At one meeting last year we asked for and answered unsigned questions from the management group; we shall continue the procedure this year at one of our meetings.

We have other plans to build up our management team, some of which will take us two or three years to work out, and we are getting results. We are just concluding a plant rehabilitation program in which we have spent an amount representing, for us, a tremendous sum ($85 million, which is nearly eight times the net value of our plant account eight years ago). Our expectations from the new equipment will not be realized, however, until we get the operating people to run it as it should be run. This is a problem in human relations which we can solve only through the management group. It is our intention to delegate to the manufacturing executives down the line the job of making this equipment work. The job involves the delegation of authority and the fixing of responsibility, and it will require every bit of help that we at the top can give.

From the Plant Superintendent's Point of View

*By William E. Collar**

Two years ago I was handed the job of starting a new manufacturing plant. It was in this job that I appreciated the full importance and the problems of effective delegation and control. If it is true that one learns from his mistakes, I have had many opportunities to learn. What I learned about delegation and control of responsibilities in setting up this plant is the basis of my discussion here.

The new plant was established in a small town in Indiana. The operation was basically a manufacturing one, producing fractional-horsepower electric motors. As plant superintendent, I had a staff of supervisors for production, quality control, industrial relations, and industrial methods. Engineering, sales, purchasing, and accounting were handled at the division headquarters. The supervisory people were experienced men taken from the home division; but it was decided that the line foremen as well as some 350 workers were to be new men from the immediate area. As our foremen we wanted men with good technical training but not necessarily with training in foremanship. We recognized that we would not have the experience that could be gained by staffing the plant with foremen from other plants. On the other hand, we would have men who were free of set habits and practices. This was particularly desirable because entirely new methods of time study and incentive payment were to be put in effect.

Some three months before the plant was to be completed, 10 foremen were hired. For over two months, five days a week, eight hours a day, they were put through a training program. This program consisted of a rather standard curriculum for foreman training

* Mr. Collar is a Plant Superintendent for Westinghouse Electric Corporation. He became associated with Westinghouse in 1942 in engineering design work and in 1949 was transferred to manufacturing. He assumed his present responsibilities in 1952.

and detailed information about systems, procedures, and company policy.

One of the basic principles on which we operated was that the foremen should *know* their jobs; they should have the facts on the operations of the departments which they control directly. They learned about budget setup, safety regulations, quality control, production schedule procedure, routing, time study, and discipline of the employees. When formal training ended, they also learned the technical operation of the machinery and equipment, material usages, and so on. When we took the plant over from the contractor — bare walls, roof, and floor — we started installing the machinery and at the same time we started hiring a limited number of production workers. And the first motors were produced with the foremen virtually the only workers. In that way they became acquainted with the machinery. They had to know exactly what the machines could and could not do.

During formal training, personnel from company headquarters and line and staff supervisors from divisional headquarters were constantly involved in teaching, telling, answering, explaining, and answering again the questions of these 10 men. I, too, was involved in the training; for the entire period I was adviser, teacher, and companion to the trainees. Through this close relationship these men came to regard me as an authority who could and would answer their every question. When the formal training period ended, we moved overnight from this status to a staff and line organization where delegation and control were to function. What happened? I delegated just as I should and I had *perfect* control — according to the textbooks. Not one of those 10 men would do anything until he had a definite *yes* or *no* from me!

The plans and schedules for going into operation were completely and carefully established. Each foreman knew what was to be accomplished, and each was aware of his own responsibilities. Yet there remained the urgent problem of getting the foremen to take action on their own initiative.

What is the reason that we did not get acceptance of the responsibilities that we delegated? Looking back on this situation I can much better evaluate it than I could at the time. I suppose it is only natural that such a group of men were reluctant to go ahead on their own immediately after a training program wherein they had been given the answers to all of their questions. Technically they were qualified to carry out their assignments. They had been instructed in the procedures and the use of operational forms; they had run the gamut of quality control, budget control, production scheduling, and human relations; and yet these men still lacked something. What they lacked was a real willingness to accept delegated responsibilities.

Gradually I realized that we had failed to build in them confidence that they as individuals were capable of arriving at final and accurate decisions. It became apparent that they were overly concerned with keeping in line with company policy. Every problem or situation was something new and different requiring a policy decision from me, whereas actually most of the problems had only to be worked out with common sense in line with existing policy.

So far I have merely described a situation where effective delegation and control were vital but did not exist. To summarize this situation: The foremen wanted to and could carry out their assignment. They had been provided with complete, detailed procedures, rules, regulations, and company policies to follow. But they lacked willingness to answer the daily problems that arose. They were laboring under the assumption that the answers to all their problems were in the rule book. Of course the answers were not all there. Failing to find the answers, instead of going ahead and working out common-sense solutions in the light of company policy, they rationalized that a new situation had arisen which would require a higher-level, policy decision.

It was only through excellent guidance from my superior and a lot of trial and error on my part that effective delegation and control were finally realized.

As long as I was willing to relieve the foremen of their responsibility, they had no need to take the initiative. This sounds very elemental in the telling. But I believe that mine is the most frequent practical failure in administration. In so many cases it is easier for the supervisor simply to give the answers than it is for him to guide the individual to reach his own decisions. Certainly a good supervisor must be willing to understand, discuss, guide, and even give advice to his people. But he must also refrain from giving them specific answers to specific problems. Once I realized my weakness in this area, I consciously concentrated on helping the foremen make their own decisions. Because of their lack of experience they needed close supervision; but close supervision does not mean making their decisions for them.

In working with these men and refusing to give the answers, I talked with them concerning their problems. Invariably the question arose whether the solution or action they were considering would violate company policy or set an undesirable precedent. They recognized that I as their supervisor would judge their performance on the basis of their ability to make decisions and to take action that stayed within the prescribed limitations. In other words, they were vitally concerned with the controls that were established for the plant. The intensive training these men were given had certainly acquainted them with these limitations. As a whole this group was well versed in the written policy and procedures governing the operations, almost to the point of having them memorized. The problem seemed to take two forms:

(1) The men had been given the policies cut-and-dried, and they were looking to them for specific answers to every question which came up.

(2) Because of the vast amount of attention that had been given to these policies and regulations, the men constantly feared making a mistake.

The problems and the situation I have discussed are not meant to be a derogatory reflection on the foremen. They are simply a realistic examination of conditions connected with delegation and control. For the record, these men started installing machinery in January, produced the first motor on April 17, and produced 20,000 motors in December — at a profit.

The point is, rather, that in our training zeal we had overemphasized the written controls upon the operation. The men needed to be given a feeling of confidence that they were capable of making satisfactory decisions. This took diligent effort on my part and the co-operation of my staff in guiding these men to make their decisions. We went out of our way to recognize and commend proper decisions. With a new group of men such as this the process was rather long and tedious, and it was hindered by another factor inherent in any organization but particularly in a new operation — the fact that as we moved along and began to develop an ability to work confidently within the company policies, we were plagued with the necessity for changing these policies and regulations.

This constant adjustment of the company ground rules to meet the distinctive realities of the particular operation offset the ability of the men to gain firm confidence in their own competence. Of course, it is impossible to establish controls that never need changing. I could have made many of these changes quickly and simply myself, but I concluded that it was highly desirable to have the foremen a part of the actual policy-making body. So a weekly meeting was held with the foremen to work out and establish new operational policies. This plan served three important purposes. First, it made clear that policies were not sacred cows but real aids to common-sense decision making. Secondly, it gave the men a feeling of responsibility for the operation. Finally, it assured me that the foremen not only were well acquainted with the letter of the rules but also had a working understanding of them.

Mr. Hanley has mentioned that his company makes a realistic attempt to include the plant manager in the development of overall company policy. In my opinion, this is a commendable effort.

Occasionally a policy decision is handed down to the plant manager level as a directive. Under such conditions a workable understanding of the policy and its purpose is not possible, and poor delegation results. This principle applies equally to decisions taken at all levels in an organization. To be effective, a decision should be made by those responsible for its execution.

With the continuation of the procedures I have outlined to you, the foremen in time became self-reliant, responsible links in the line organization. Study of the things which were done leads to the conclusion that a step-by-step policy can be worked out for effective delegation and control at the plant level.

The foremen training program we set up was not perfect, and when we had to go into a second shift and were faced with the same problem again, we made certain changes on the basis of our experience. We proceeded by selecting the foremen exactly as we had selected the first group. But, instead of spending a whole day in class, the new men worked with a foreman on the floor in the morning; and in the afternoon they attended classes on procedures and forms, and the technical aspects of their jobs. One day a week the existing line foremen presented actual problems they had had recently which applied to the subject the trainees were studying in class that week. The new men got a chance to work on real problems of the kind they would face and learned to come to decisions on them. And they proved to be far less reluctant to accept authority and responsibility when these were finally delegated to them.

In looking back on the problems and solutions, the thought occurs to me that delegating and controlling seem to be upside down. Doesn't it make more sense to speak of controlling the delegated responsibilities than delegating and controlling responsibilities? I believe that the underlying problem in this situation was that the individuals did not have a basic, workable understanding of the controls to be used in establishing the operation. Rather they had a highly technical knowledge of the written policy.

Most of us who have been in our jobs for some time know what we wish to accomplish. We know within what limits of company policy this must be accomplished. We know to what extent we will regulate or adjust company rules to allow this to be accomplished. We know how much money we are willing to spend to have this accomplished. We know these things which we use to establish controls over the operations of those people to whom we delegate responsibility. What better way, then, to obtain good control than to give this same understanding to those people to whom we delegate responsibility?

Too many of us formally delegate responsibility and then grope around for ways to control it. This sequence leads to a feeling of frustration on the part of our subordinates and lack of confidence in their own ability to make decisions. To summarize my beliefs garnered from this experience of setting up a plant, here are five criteria for effective delegation to and control of any subordinate:

(1) *He must know what is expected of him.* This is the first step, and I believe we in industry generally do a good job on it.

(2) *He must be physically and technically capable of carrying out his assignment.* With the resources the American educational system provides and with the developing emphasis in industry on training, this rule is becoming easier to follow.

(3) *He must know that his superior understands his problems and that he can get guidance and advice but that he cannot get the answers.* This rule is widely broken; many times we delegate responsibility and then eliminate that responsibility by taking the action ourselves.

(4) *He must not only know in a formal sense what his limits are as far as company policy, regulations, and his personal responsibility go; he must also understand them.* This will serve to give the individual vital self-confidence. If he thoroughly understands the controls at the time the delegation is made, he is in a position to reach decisions that are compatible with company objectives and he is emotionally willing to make such decisions.

(5) *He must know that whenever changes in the ground rules are necessary, he will have an active role in formulating them, where this is possible.* At the least, he should understand the purpose as well as the letter of the new controls. Otherwise frequent and arbitrary changing of the rules will cause a feeling of frustration and also a lack of confidence.

To Outside Organizations

*By Frank G. Chambers**

Delegation of responsibility and control of performance in manufacturing enterprises are traditionally considered internal functions

* Mr. Chambers is Vice President — Manufacturing of Magna Engineering Corporation. He was previously associated with R. H. Macy & Co., Inc. In 1947 he and two others organized Magna Engineering which produces the "Shopsmith" multipurpose power tool.

—part of the administration of a company's own staff. Our company learned, quite by happenstance and evolution, that responsibility can be delegated to outside organizations in substantially the same way that it is delegated to one's own employees. We are now devoted believers in the effectiveness and desirability of this technique. It has been a key policy in permitting us to grow rapidly.

Let me present my observations in the form of a case study. The vital statistics required to understand and evaluate our performance are these:

(1) Three people—an engineer-inventor and two decidedly inexperienced graduates of the Harvard Business School—established a company in 1947 to develop, manufacture, and distribute a woodworking power tool.

(2) The funds available were only our wartime personal savings.

(3) Our manufacturing knowledge was nil.

(4) We had no plant facilities.

(5) Our objective was to set up a company of our own which would provide a livelihood, rapid growth, a capacity for developing a secure market position, and an intellectual challenge.

In recognition of these facts, we established what we now realize was crash-schedule timing. From March to June, we converted a design idea into a finished product—a power tool which retailed for nearly $200. Simultaneously we developed our marketing policies and manufacturing plans. In July, we displayed our prototype to what we had decided was to be our key retail account—Montgomery Ward. By August, Montgomery Ward was convinced that the product had merit, and that our enthusiasm and confidence were sufficient to overcome our lack of funds and manufacturing know-how. In September, we placed a contract for manufacture with a large but hungry ship-repair company. In mid-November, we delivered our first 250 machines precisely on the schedule we had promised. Thus was established our initial confidence in delegation of responsibility to an outside organization.

Subsequently we added a second manufacturing source to provide more capacity and insurance against the failure of one. The results were equally satisfactory. Until the Korean crisis, all manufacturing was "delegated" to outside organizations. Korea caused a profound change in our situation. We had to insure our source of supply against possible sale of the plants in the rapidly rising market for machine tools and manufacturing buildings. We therefore purchased the plant which had been producing for us in California. This move made it necessary to reappraise our previous manufacturing policy.

Despite the fact that we now owned plant facilities, we concluded that delegation to outside organizations had worked so well that it should be continued except where there was no suitable facility available or none capable of being developed, or where uneconomic movement of materials would be required. This policy has remained a conviction, not a secondary objective; we now pay four dollars to outside organizations for each dollar spent for labor in our own plant.

The reader might quite logically ask: Why is this delegation? Isn't your practice merely one of the answers to the time-honored question *make or buy?* My answer is *no*. The difference lies in the approach itself, the techniques of delegation and control employed, and in the integration of purchasing and manufacturing into the over-all organization plan. Furthermore, real delegation is involved in our relations with only 12 of the 300 suppliers from whom we purchase.

In deciding whether to use an outside organization or to perform a given operation in our own plant, we do not make price or availability of equipment or space the first consideration. We first appraise the character and qualifications of our own manufacturing supervisory staff and those of potential outside suppliers. We attempt to evaluate the amount of effort which each will concentrate on the specific task. We compare the incentive which will drive each individual on the project. And when a decision is made to use an outside organization, the negotiations are carefully keyed to make it clear that we are delegating responsibility, not merely placing an order for material. We are, in fact, buying management—specialized management of higher qualifications than our staff has.

Specifically, this is the way we proceed once we have determined that a function is to be performed outside. We develop a list of all potential suppliers located in the geographic area that can be closely administered — in our case the state of California. (It is two flying hours from our headquarters to Los Angeles, with hourly plane schedules; and there is also good overnight train service.) We procure Dun and Bradstreet reports on each and use such other investigatory means as we may need in order to feel well informed on size of the supplier's organization, the reputation of the management, the age of the operating individuals, and financial status. Usually, two men of our staff then visit the most likely prospects. Each is studied with five criteria in mind:

(1) *Is the reputation of the owners or operators (preferably the same men) publicly satisfactory; and is there evidence of success as manufacturers?* This does not mean that we look for old and established companies. Quite the contrary; we are far more likely to find our answer in a young, striving company with much to gain from affiliating with us. The earmarks of previous accomplishment, however, must be there, since our plan is akin to adding a new member to our staff.

(2) *Is there a deep interest in, and desire to keep up with, technical progress?* The answer to this question can be discovered by going forearmed with a question about a new process or machine reported in a technical journal. To be satisfactory, each major supplier must take the responsibility not only for continued economical manufacture, but also for being a major source of technical education for our own engineers and plant staff.

(3) *Does the potential supplier have a strong desire to become part of our organization?* We do not look for just an expression of interest in our volume of business, but a voluntary indication of willingness to take the difficult manufacturing along with the easy, to face tough quality-determination problems with the attitude that the real consideration is what the ultimate consumer wants, whether that be sensible or frivolous. The sincerity of the desire to accept responsibility for giving us what is needed on a permanent basis is often the deciding factor in the selection of a supplier.

(4) *Is the supplier responsive to incentives which are within our ability to offer?* Specifically, is our volume of business sufficient to

make us a large enough customer to affect his profit noticeably? We prefer to have our business 20 to 40 per cent of the supplier's volume—not over 50 per cent certainly, and yet large enough so that there is no one in the supplying firm who is not aware of it. Would our volume help him to grow, to replace equipment, to improve operating techniques? Would we help in his diversification objectives? We find out if freedom from certain annoyances customarily present in the buying relationship would be recognized and appreciated. We can also offer some freedom from never-ending sales responsibilities. Scheduling under the delegation plan can best be done by telephone with our supplier's manufacturing people rather than through his salesmen. Often we have been able to provide financial assistance in the form of working capital to carry the burden of our work-in-process. And finally, we can offer the incentive of a court of last resort. No supplier need stop at the director of purchasing should he feel aggrieved. Without prejudice he has the privilege of contact with the owners of the company. This has often proved to have an especially strong appeal.

(5) *Does the potential supplier have a thorough understanding of consumer goods economics?* This criterion was added when we found from somewhat sad experience that organizations with only capital goods experience follow courses of price adjustment incompatible with our relative inflexibility to change selling prices.

Once a "delegation" supplier has been selected, using the procedure just outlined, his thorough education is undertaken. There are six recognized parts of this program:

(1) We arrange for the owner-operators to visit our plant and offices for a general discussion of our program and sales prospects. We always make certain that the manufacturer knows how his parts will fit into our machine and into our merchandising program.

(2) We see that the newly selected supplier knows a number of people in the company—not just the men with whom he will work most directly. At present, our dozen major contract manufacturers know the key men in our sales organization, the design engineers, and often even the accounting staff. Every effort is made to keep this contact informal and social.

(3) Our purchasing staff, manufacturing supervisors, engineers, and our three owner-operators frequently visit the plant of each major supplier. This leads to camaraderie and also develops ideas which ultimately lower the prices we pay. In this way we make a conscientious effort to know the problems of each major supplier.

(4) The director of purchasing religiously prepares letters of commendation for superior performance by suppliers. Whenever a difficult schedule is met, whenever a price is reduced through improved methods or clever engineering, or whenever any out-of-the-way performance comes to his attention, he dispatches a letter recognizing the accomplishment. From the excellent reaction to this technique, I am surprised at the apparent rarity of its use in other organizations.

(5) Important sales literature and advertisements are always sent to suppliers just as they are to retail stores to whom we sell. Such materials are constant reminders and customarily are posted on bulletin boards in suppliers' plants. This further helps to identify us and even to sell our product.

(6) We make certain that "delegation" suppliers have "inside" information. We stage formal advance presentations of new models especially for them. Such presentations are so uncommon that their effect is magnified well beyond their cost. We also are careful to invite the "delegation" suppliers to some of our company social affairs.

Working contact with and direction of the "delegation" suppliers is through the director of purchasing (who is on the same level as the manager of manufacturing). The methods of communication used and the attitudes which prevail are identical with those used and prevailing in administration of our own staff. Several of the suppliers provide us with operations sheets and cost studies on their own initiative. We in turn give all 12 "delegation" suppliers our yearly production estimates by months.

Every year we review each supplier by a method comparable to a salary adjustment conference for a company executive. Successes and failures are listed and fully discussed, as is the total amount of work performed. We want the supplier to realize how much our total volume has been, that we have a long memory for failures, that we recognize extraordinary co-operation. These meetings have led to cost studies which have bettered prices, and they also have established tighter bonds of co-operation.

A clearer picture of our delegation technique may result if a few actual cases are outlined.

Early in our history we went in search of a screw-machine product plant which would be large enough to have the most elaborate equipment in use, large enough to meet heavy peak loads, and in a position to buy mill quantities of steel and aluminum even in times of tight supply. Only one plant on the West Coast met this test. The assurance that we obtain all of our screw-machine parts from this supplier has built such co-operation that the men who manage operations there have never failed us. They estimate on new parts merely by sending us their operations sheets with the times involved. Their production manager has proposed engineering changes — not only in the parts they make but also in other parts — which have saved us thousands of dollars.

This company, located 500 miles from our plant, will assist in obtaining information and deliveries from smaller suppliers located near it, and, in fact, will do anything to further our mutual interests. It will not object to adverse quality-control decisions but will do everything possible to see that our operation runs smoothly. We could well justify a screw-machine department of substantial size, but we could never rival the satisfactory, trouble-free management relationship we now enjoy. When we changed the design of our power tool early this year, this supplier presented his new prices with this foreword:

"Pricing of a manufactured article, whether it be a complete unit or a single component, is an ever-changing and variable thing. To maintain a successful relationship between the producer of components and the ultimate manufacturer requires constant scrutiny of the pricing formula to afford to the manufacturer the quality, price, and service he requires to maintain his production and at the same time afford to the manufacturer of the component a profitable operation.

"Recognizing price is a primary requisite, we have endeavored to review our history of the various components, readjust and afford to you savings that have been realized, and wherever necessary readjust where the pricing has given to us a negative figure.

"We feel that such a review is mandatory and it is our intention to review the performance of the parts in production on a semiannual basis.

"We here feel a very definite responsibility to Magna and we trust the summary sheets following are received and accepted as the best we can do at this time, recognizing and firmly believing that additional savings will accrue as added experience is acquired and stabilization of design is accomplished."

Another example of delegation involves a portion of our painting function. Our redesigned tool used four large stampings which had to be painted the same color and texture as the machine itself. Since we were adding to our own in-plant painting facilities, we could readily have decided to finish the stampings. We concluded, however, that the task could be advantageously delegated to the stamper. He had no painting equipment but jumped at the suggestion that he do the work. He installed many thousands of dollars' worth of equipment, and he has relieved our own plant of a materials handling problem. The stamping plant is a 60-man organization with a single owner-operator. His costs are well below what it would have cost us to do the work in our plant, and we obtain what we want from him more easily than we would from our own painting department supervisor. He will experiment, he will work overtime, and he will accept responsibility with far less explanation than is typical of most directly administered employees.

Not every delegation is successful, of course. An example of failure was an effort to work with a large eastern producer of powdered iron parts. This company would accept little responsibility. Its executives resisted efforts to establish a co-operative liaison. We were a customer, they a supplier, and they would not be a member of a team. Eventually we searched for a new answer. We located a California plant manufacturing house door locks which had a small experimental powdered iron operation under way to make components for its own product. We arranged for a demonstration of our power tool to its executive staff and succeeded in instilling enthusiasm in them. The result has been exceptionally satisfactory. They now operate exactly as a department of our own manufacturing plant. They engage in extensive and expensive experimental work. They accept responsibility for finding a working answer—not just producing what our drawings specify.

Still another instance of delegation is our die-casting supply. The plant we purchased had done its own die-casting, and the conventional answer would have been to expand the captive operation to care for the new workload. Investigation showed us, however, that there are many specialties within the die-casting field. Consequently we now use four different companies, each a specialist. We range in size as a customer from 10 per cent to 50 per cent of their sales volume. Our peak loads are well distributed. Competition between them is vigorous yet friendly. All have been of great engineering service whenever we have designed new items using die-castings. Our costs are doubtless well below what we could ever have accomplished in a captive plant—and we do not even need a full-time buyer of die-cast parts.

We undoubtedly could learn to make many of the products made outside in our own plant if we wanted to, but, fundamentally, we do not believe that there is a double profit to be made. We think that we can buy far more skill, the use of far more elaborate equipment, the freedom from far more problems (including the problems of peak loads), and overhead rates below what would apply in our own plant if we work hard enough with these large "delegation" suppliers and their accounting departments.

We are convinced that not only do they not cost us more but the parts that we buy outside actually cost us considerably less than if we made them ourselves. We never give serious consideration today to die-casting, to screw-machine parts manufacture, or to stamping in our own plant. It is our experience that costs are lower with delegation in a booming market as well as in a time of some contraction.

The reader may well wonder why, if the technique is desirable, we do not use it 100 per cent. The reason is that not all of our operations meet the requirements or are suitable. The technique is applicable only where a manufacturer has his own designed product, where there is substantial tooling involved, and — most important — where the management can afford to devote the energy required in working with a supplier in this close way. We could perhaps increase one dozen "delegation" suppliers to 25, but I do not think we could carry out the program for a number of suppliers much beyond that.

Delegation to outside organizations may be a worth-while area in which others can experiment. It is one way to make a big business in terms of sales out of a relatively small investment. The distinction between it and conventional relations with suppliers may seem very narrow, but we believe it to be significant.

This kind of delegation has made it possible for us to have a flexibility we could not attain within our own four walls. We expect to achieve sales volume in the coming year of $9 million, with 350 employees. The dozen contract manufacturers to whom we delegate will employ almost the same number doing our work. Our costs are most surely low. Delegating authority and responsibility to suppliers has been one of the most important single factors behind the ability of Magna to grow quickly in a highly competitive field from a starting point at which the company was almost completely lacking in resources and facilities.

EFFECTIVE DELEGATION AND CONTROL BY THE CONTROLLER

Introduction

*By Robert N. Anthony**

The general subject of delegation and control by the controller is such a big one that for the purposes of this chapter we propose to focus on one specific area: the implications of electronic data-processing equipment on the control function and on the controller.

Let me begin by calling your attention to two dates, less than 10 years apart. The first date is August 1944, when the first large-scale digital computing machine in existence went into operation at the Harvard Computation Laboratory. The second date is April 1954, when the first large-scale *office* data-processing machine went into operation at the Louisville plant of the General Electric Company. The rapid development that has taken place in this brief 10-year span has made it apparent that data-processing equipment will have a tremendous impact on the control function in American business, although we have no idea as yet as to exactly what form this impact will take.

Two of the men who will discuss the problem in this chapter are associated with the key dates mentioned above. Professor Howard Aiken was in charge of the original installation in 1944, and for his work then and subsequently he can justifiably be called the father of electronic computers. Mr. Roddy Osborn is in charge of the General Electric installation at Louisville. Mr. John Haslett writes from his own experience of analyzing the application of the data-processing equipment to the Shell Oil Company.

* Mr. Anthony, who served as moderator of the panel session on which this chapter is based, is Associate Professor of Business Administration, Harvard Business School.

The State of the Art of Electronic Computers

*A Paraphrase**

It is impossible to have any clear idea of what is going to happen with the computing machine during the next few years without first looking at what has gone on in the past, and also at the state of the art at the present time.

Everyone who was in any way connected with the original development of large-scale computers had in mind only one thing—namely, the construction of machines for the solution of *scientific* problems. There was no expectation that these machines were ultimately going to be instruments which could be used for control in business. The sole aim was to solve differential equations, the problems of physics and aircraft design. These problems involved the controlling type of variable that led to the design and construction of the machines which are now in the Computation Laboratory at Harvard.

The concept of the computer is really very simple. You provide yourself with a lot of registers in which you can store numbers. You provide yourself with something that can add, something that can subtract, something else that can multiply and divide. You take all the pieces of equipment, and connect them together by means of an electronic system so that they can communicate one with another. Then you can control a sequence, a transfer of numbers from one place to another, in accordance with a certain pattern that is dictated by the problem under consideration. And the machine leads to the solution of the problem.

Now, the success achieved in this field of scientific computation is such that any man who ever again computes by hand the entries

* This chapter section represents the extemporaneous remarks of Professor Howard H. Aiken as paraphrased by the Editor. Professor Aiken is Director of the Computation Laboratory, Harvard University, and has designed and supervised the building of four large-scale digital computing machines, including the first one ever to be put in operation.

of a mathematical table, as a result of the application of scientific formulas, is wasting a certain fragment of his lifetime while he does it. Such is the success of the scientific computer that manual labor in this direction can be abandoned.

So far, so good. But how does this lead us to the point where we begin to wonder whether the computer can be used in business? How about the concept of the general automatic office? Where does it come in?

The first observation that can be made on this is that scientific computation makes use of the four fundamental rules of arithmetic — adding, subtracting, multiplying, and dividing; accounting uses the same rules. Also, in scientific computations, you have to store up certain numbers while you do something arithmetical with certain other numbers, then you recombine them, and so on. Accounting follows exactly the same procedure. Therefore, since there is already available a computer for solving scientific problems, why can it not be applied to the solution of accounting problems as well?

From an arithmetic point of view, fundamentally, there is absolutely no reason why this could not be done. But, when you start examining the property of these machines — the peripheral equipment, the input equipment, the output equipment, and so on — you will find that there can be vast differences in accounting and scientific applications.

It is this basic observation (the fact that accounting methods and scientific computations both use the same kind of arithmetical elements) which has led to the great amount of discussion about the application of computing devices to accounting problems, with the result that there is considerable confusion. For instance, at one meeting a distinguished speaker says that electronics is here, right now; that we have the machines, and we have the philosophy and everything else that it takes to do this job. Then a week or two later at another meeting an equally distinguished speaker throws cold water on the whole thing; he is disturbed, he has not been able to see how he could cut costs and do the job. How is it that two equally reasonable people come to completely divergent points of view as the result of examining the same kind of apparatus?

One man is thinking about scientific or mathematical computations which have to do with forecasting, statistics, and a great variety of mathematical procedures, and their applications to data necessary for making a decision on how you should run a business.

The computations needed for such statistical investigations that deal with commercial data are exactly the same kind of computations needed for data in nuclear physics. Thus, from the standpoint of linear programing, statistical analysis, and any kind of computations of a mathematical character that are useful in helping to operate a business, there is no question but that electronic computing machinery is applicable.

Moreover, there is no question but that the machines already produced are adequate to undertake these tasks; and, insofar as the basic mathematical principles are concerned, there is no reason not to be using this machinery at the present moment. The man who says that electronics is ready for business to use starts with this kind of activity in mind.

The other man, by contrast, is thinking about such things as turning out 50,000 customer bills per day for a public utility. Can such operations be carried out on a large scale on a commercially available computer? The existing machinery may not be the best that can be conceived of to do the job, even with the addition of special devices to prepare bills. The particular routines necessary for extensive payroll operations may be best handled, not by large-scale computers, but by lesser equipment of a single-purpose character.

In regard to the almost unbounded interest in computing machines, one limitation can be placed on what they are able to do.

It is certainly true that if we design appropriate computing and logical machines, we should be able to reduce the flow of information through these machines to one path. But as yet there are no devices to translate a piece of information to mechanical form. We must still go through a keying, or coding, operation for each set of data that we introduce. And in the absence of such devices we are still "stuck," in the sense of not being able to get full value out of the computer's speed and accuracy.

The question is — thinking about the next 10 years — whether we will ever have devices that can read original source documents and convert data to holes in the tape or to binary digits or something of that kind. Actually, there is a good deal of activity and some progress in this field.

If the problem were reduced to the state where paper of one size and uniform type face were always used — in other words, if the same kind of pattern were always followed — designing a machine to read that paper and hole it in the cards would be possible.

However, as soon as there is any variation from one document to another, the problem becomes more difficult. Differences between type faces are bad enough; trying to read handwriting mechanically is almost impossible.

All of this means that in many industries and in many endeavors, the cost of the machinery and the rapidity with which specialized machinery can be developed could be greatly reduced with the aid of standard procedures. Thus, as it is now, banks have to handle different sizes and different colors of checks, different locations of numbers and amounts on the checks, to the extent that it is almost impossible to conceive of a machine that would read any check and transfer the information to a mechanical device. However, a simple decision on the part of management that all checks should be of the same size and the same kind of type (or within a reasonable degree of variation) would help enormously in leading the way to mechanization and simplifying the flow of information involved.

Still another point that should be understood and emphasized is this: in the last analysis, *no computing machine can do for a person anything that he cannot think through himself.*

It is true that the computing machine, because of its great power and speed, can accomplish things that a person would not live long enough to do, if he did not have a machine. But so far as *how* operations are to be done, a person has to be completely able to know and plan this for the machine, because it cannot function otherwise.

A further point to keep in mind in connection with the use of electronic computers is that, when machines are applied to carry out operations that were previously handled manually, in all probability there will be changes in the operations.

The tools which one uses for carrying out any piece of work affect, at least in part, the nature of the product turned out. To illustrate this point, suppose you are given a saw and a hammer and asked to build a house. You would build a frame house, whether that is the kind of house wanted or not. Actually there is no question but that it would be a frame house, because of the kind of tools that you have to work with. However, if you are given a trowel and asked to build a house, you will probably produce a masonry house because a trowel does not lend itself to any other kind of building.

Or consider the case of a manufacturer of plastic parts. He designs a little piece of something and gives a drawing to the production manager, who goes ahead and makes a sample and brings it back to him. In the main, that sample is what he wants. But perhaps he finds in the sample four or five dents that he did not want and a hole in there somewhere that he did not specify. So, he says to the production manager, "Why did you do that?" And the latter replies: "I did it because I didn't think you would object to those features, and by putting them in, I can make this gadget for you economically; whereas, if you do not want them in there, it will cost you a dollar instead of six cents."

By the same token, machinery cannot be expected to carry out in the same way the operations which are presently done in offices by manual means. There are certain things now being done that must be changed in order to facilitate the operation. Also, there are certain other things that machines can now do for you, which you would like them to do, but which you cannot take advantage of because the cost is too great.

At least there must be give-and-take on the part of those conducting the operations of the system, if the machines are to go into operation. And, unless you are willing to study the machinery itself enough to know the concessions you will have to make, you will not reap the rewards available to you from those possibilities.

If there is any one fallacy which has ever been uttered in connection with automatic machinery, at least from the point of view of people who wish to operate the machines, it is that there is something about the machines that makes them almost think. Not to be philosophical, but so far as data processing and techniques are concerned, that is pure nonsense.

An exercise in syllogisms points up the fallacy:

> The dictionary lists many meanings and connotations for the verb "to think." But just because a machine can do many of the things that are listed there — like multiplying and remembering — does not mean that it can think; slide rules can multiply and books can remember, but they do not think. Neither does the fact that carrying out routines by itself mean that the computer can think; automatic screw machines can do as much. And as far as being able to make choices, there are more electrical goings-on that make choices to get your number when you dial a telephone than there are in any computing machine.
>
> In short, you have only to pursue the notion that the machine thinks, and you talk yourself into saying that the mechanical devices that make up our industrial civilization are all thinking machines. And you also get to a point where you have no simple verb left to represent those processes in the mind of a man who directs the machines.

This all leads to a question that is frequently asked, whether there is any possibility of developing decision-making machinery. And here is what really can be done. Any operation or sequence of operations that men can design in the laboratory, they can make a machine to do. But there is no process of logic whatsoever that men can design in the laboratory. Logic is the thinking that cannot be mechanized.

In regard to making decisions, every computing machine will do what you want it to do. As pointed out by Mr. Osborn in the following section, it will require 30 man-years to get his system at General Electric into operation, and at least 24 of those will be spent in thinking out the system that is wanted; the remaining 6 are enough to figure out how to do it. It is those first 24 years that show that man must do the thinking. After you have completed the thinking, you can program the decisions; there is no problem here. But making the decisions is an entirely different matter. To illustrate, if *a, b,* and *c* are desirable and if you know that a certain conclusion is to be reached when *a, b,* and *c* are together, you can tell the machine: "If ever you get all three of these factors at one time, then you are to take the following action." But you cannot say to the machine: "When certain conditions arise, you make the best decision."

No! Man must do the thinking—decide what he means and recognize it. Then the computer will make the decision according to the formula that man has worked out for it.

It is for this reason that the computing machines belong in the category of *useful tools.* Forego this notion of "thinking" machinery; leave that idea to the philosophers and to those who wish to study the comparison of computing machines with the nervous system.

If we can get further and further away from this notion of thinking machines and realize that we have to do the thinking, that we have to understand the problem and know how to program the computing machine to make a sales forecast, then the computing machine will be a highly useful tool to help us get the job done. And that's about all.

It may sound as though the machine is being debunked; and perhaps it should be debunked just a little.

But it isn't the machine itself that really needs to be debunked, because there is much that can be expected of computing machines. During the next 10 years, we are going to see ever more powerful, logical machinery tending in the direction of the automatic office, and even in the direction of the automatic factory. However, it is going to be accomplished by virtue of *man's* thought, and not the thinking of the machine.

Management Implications of Data-Processing Equipment

*By Roddy F. Osborn**

I wish to include in this section some ideas regarding the impact that our available electronic data-processing equipment will have on the controller and on the office. I shall highlight some of the results or soon-to-be-realized results of our attempts to use such equipment at the Major Appliance Division of General Electric Company.

Electronic data-processing equipment can serve all phases of management as a means of delegation, communication, control, and measurement. Indeed it will, in my opinion, soon come to be recognized as the most powerful management tool ever invented.

Within the framework of a properly designed computer program, the controller can be assured that his instructions are carried out explicitly — no longer subject to individual interpretation, intuition, or experience.

As a communicating device the computer can serve in gathering, summarizing, interpreting, and using all information at all levels of corporate activity. By processing all data relating to the business — by doing it in an integrated manner and by doing it accurately, intelligently, and promptly — electronic data-processing equipment will provide the controller with the information necessary to make more timely and informed decisions, and will simultaneously provide an efficient, integrated communications system for all levels of management.

Control can be exercised through the ability of the system to sift the important from the unimportant and provide an editing of all business transactions. The typical summaries of information reaching the controller today frequently hide the details needed for

* Mr. Osborn is Manager–Business Procedures, Major Appliance Division, General Electric Company, Louisville, Kentucky. Since November 1951, he has been responsible for putting business' first large-scale office data-processing machine into operation at the Louisville plant.

executive action; but, with electronic data-processing systems, reports needed at all levels of management can be promptly condensed without loss of detail and without duplication of effort.

Measurement can be accomplished automatically for all levels of the company's activities through automatic comparisons with pre-established standards and ratios, adjusted as changing conditions require.

The management implications of computers harnessed to business literally stagger the imagination. Some indication of the impact on controllers was expressed in a speech by Joseph B. Jeming, a New York consultant, when he addressed the Controllers' Institute of America on October 1, 1951:

> "The electronic accounting system will not be seen until the vision, initiative, and self-interest of the controllers start the ball rolling. The first electronic accounting system will take time and money and a great deal of planning. How soon the first system can be seen depends not on the business machine companies and not on the engineers but on the controllers themselves. One thing is certain; the first electronic accounting system which goes into operation anywhere will start the revolution in every accounting office and every controller should be forearmed for it."

The revolution to which Mr. Jeming refers has now begun at our new Appliance Park near Louisville, Kentucky, with the first harnessing of a giant brain to the day-to-day problems of a large manufacturing plant. Indeed, it may well come to pass that the first union of modern manufacturing and the electronic computer will be remembered as a milestone in our progress comparable to the concept of mass production. It is quite possible that Appliance Park may eventually be recorded by historians as the birthplace of the second industrial revolution.

Consider the increased potential of the controller's function with portions of his work carried on by electronic computers as we plan to use them:

1. The computing of incentive pay, gross pay, deductions, and net pay for approximately 12,000 employees, including distribution to appropriate cost accounts, in two hours weekly; the printing of pay checks, pay

registers, personnel reports, cost accounting entries, in another four hours weekly — all accomplished without error. Our timetable: the first computer payroll operating in September 1954.

2. The explosion of production schedules, within minutes, into detailed material requirements by days and weeks for any given period. Inventory balances maintained by posting daily receipts and withdrawals; open orders on vendors recorded and adjusted daily. Proposed production schedules analyzed to determine the extent to which they can be satisfied by present inventories and inventory commitments. Our timetable for this is October 1954.

3. Orders from distributors processed electronically to prepare shipping schedules, invoices, sales, and cost-of-sales entries.

4. The output from these three applications combined with journal entries to produce general and special ledgers, reports, balance sheets, profit and loss statements.

5. Annual, quarterly, monthly, weekly budgets prepared in 15 to 20 minutes, with the possibility of including in the revisions last week's information (or even yesterday's) on variances in labor and material. Through this process we have a feedback of information similar to the feedback concept in the automatic factory.

6. The ability to analyze, through this budget application, the net-profit effect of proposed changes in production — integrated budgeting for the future. For the first time, we have an opportunity to start accounting for the future.

7. The reporting of sales and inventories at all levels of distribution, including initial phases of short-range and long-range projections and forecasts of sales and multiple correlation with economic and other factors affecting sales of our products.

8. Factory machine-loading schedules, now a 3-week job, prepared in about 15 minutes.

These objectives are all under way or expected to be accomplished by June 1955.

In the more distant future we expect to have:

1. A true application of production control, including optimum coordination of materials, machines, and labor.

2. Long-range sales forecasts, correlated with existing but inadequately used data, such as new family formations, disposable income, level of employment, competitors' activities, and so forth.

Our integrated system, when complete, is expected to provide a *dynamic distribution analysis* taking information from sales records and projections and providing management with an up-to-the-minute picture of the retail trade and a photoflash picture of our distribution pipelines to all areas of the country. Coupled with the ability to revise budgets and control production adequately, this should give management the opportunity to adjust and co-ordinate selling and factory effort to maximum advantage. With such an integrated system, the impact of this revolutionary device as a management tool becomes apparent:

1. Management by exception becomes practicable.
2. Accounting emphasis is transferred from historical reporting to accounting for the future.
3. Management for the first time should find itself able to use all the production facilities placed at its disposal with maximum effectiveness.

Perhaps there will be some interest in how we explored this field at General Electric.

First, we limited our review of equipment to that which already existed or was about to be available. We were interested only in a complete system with adequate input and output, as distinguished from a computer alone. Thus, we restricted our review to the IBM 702, which I understand will be available in December 1954, and the Univac, which was available, I believe, in 1951. However, since six of the Univac computers had been in government service and therefore tested in actual operation, and the IBM 702 was not yet available, we finally decided to give Univac first consideration.

Secondly, we started out with what we term the "limited perimeter" approach, concentrating on as small an area as possible in order to find the smallest job in which savings could be equated to the cost of this data-processing system.

Surprisingly enough, we selected only four areas of application. We found in the course of our survey that we reach the breakeven point when we have only 5,000 employees and when we use the computer only 10 per cent of the available time. (Our employment today is 5,000, and we will build it up to approximately 12,000 by 1956 when the plant is completed.)

Ten per cent of the available time is 10 hours a week. (Most of the computing systems can actually operate 168 hours, but conservatively we figure 100 usable hours.) The survey also showed that when we reach full employment and use the computer one-half of one shift and still limit its use to these four initial applications, we can expect to save approximately one-half million dollars a year.

Moreover, all this indicates that it is not necessary to be big like Shell Oil, or General Electric, or the United States Government for a company to be able to afford one of these computers. In fact, as pointed out in the *Harvard Business Review,*[1] within the next 10 years companies with as few as 500 employees will find they can afford the Univac or the 702.

Now, the results of our study would not be convincing unless we could show definitely where savings could be effected. We had to have something concrete to take to the board of directors — something that we could put a price tag on, such as fewer people required to handle payroll, material and inventory control, order service and billing, and general cost accounting.

In those areas, we found that we could replace clerical people in the routine jobs. We evaluated the savings in terms of people off the payroll, the fringe benefits, and (because our new plant was not yet complete) we also included space rental and a nominal figure for depreciation of the desks and office machines that we would have to supply to these people.

We did not reach out for additional benefits, such as those resulting from more prompt reporting or decisions based on better information. We limited ourselves to tangible dollar savings directly related to people off the payroll, and we compared these savings with the cost of operating the data-processing center, including rental, operating personnel, space, and so forth.

We have at Louisville five separate and completely decentralized departments, and operations are very diversified. There are around 700 employees in the smallest department and around 7,000 in the largest.

As you might expect, we have manual systems as well as IBM

[1] Roddy F. Osborn, "GE and UNIVAC: Harnessing the High-Speed Computer," *Harvard Business Review,* July–August 1954, p. 99; and John A. Higgins and Joseph S. Glickauf, "Electronics Down to Earth," *Harvard Business Review,* March–April 1954, p. 97.

tabulating systems. So it was in comparison with the present methods that the study revealed we could achieve savings by further intensive mechanization.

The cost of installing the data-processing equipment varies with the components required. In our particular case, the purchase cost would be $1.3 million. We have elected to rent at $20,000 a month, with an option to buy. That rental includes maintenance, service personnel, and all replacement parts required. And we have an opportunity to apply a portion of the rental toward the purchase price at a later date.

In order to put the four initial applications into effect, it will require 30 man-years of planning effort—roughly, 7 man-years each. To those readers who might not have investigated mechanization very extensively, it may be surprising to hear that 80 to 85 per cent of that time is devoted to finding out what is to be done and designing a system that will cope with it. The residual 20 to 15 per cent of the time is involved in actual computer programs and instructions for the computer. But the bulk of the job is in systems design.

But let us return to the specific subject of the chapter, "Effective Delegation and Control by Controllers."

¶ *Delegation* is found in the example of payrolls computed uniformly, accurately, quickly, with strict conformance to written instructions, labor contracts, and approved interpretations. Delegated duties are carried out precisely.

¶ Material balances are *controlled* electronically; costs are controlled through variances detected promptly, screened for importance, and reported if pertinent.

¶ Production facilities are scheduled for optimum usage, and adequately co-ordinated with market potentials, with performance measured against standards.

¶ Budgets are revised quarterly, monthly, weekly, or daily, incorporating yesterday's data into today's plans for tomorrow's action.

Thus through proper delegation, adequate communication, rigid control, and integrated measurement, the management team is released for its full potential, and the optimum use of all facilities for maximum benefit is realized.

Impact of Electronic Computers on the Controller's Job

*By John W. Haslett**

More, perhaps, than any other member of the management team will the controller increase in stature through the advent of electronic computing machines. Already this portent is becoming clear as the computers come into more widespread use for planning, coordination, and control functions. These activities being inherent in the controller's job, a tool which allows him the better to carry them out will not long be neglected.

Just as budgets, financial audits, and systems studies have brought the controller into closer integration with his management teammates, so is it inevitable that this trend will continue as electronics improves analysis, interpretation, and forecasting — not only of financial results but of operations as well. So long as integration persists and traditional departmental barriers are penetrated, a fuller potential of all levels of management will have been surely released and the leadership of the controller put to test.

Electronics presents a significant challenge to the controller, an opportunity he should not hesitate to grasp, although he may regard himself ill-prepared to do so at first. To overcome a reluctance to act he should consider a plan which has already been proved practical. This plan is one for action which the controller of any company, regardless of size, may put into effect at relatively little cost.

The plan provides a sound basis for a controller to judge for himself to what exent, if any, electronic computing machines

* Mr. Haslett is Manager, Methods and Statistics Department, Shell Oil Company. Previous to becoming associated with Shell Oil Company in 1947, he spent a brief period establishing and directing organization and methods programs for the Veterans Administration in Washington, D.C. During World War II he was a consultant to General Brehon Somervell's key management improvement group, the Control Division, Headquarters, Army Service Forces. Later as a commissioned officer, he served in a similar capacity in the office of the Chief of Transportation.

properly fit into his company's operations. Aside from his direct interest in utilizing appropriate equipment for his own accounting procedures, the controller should be able to exercise educated judgment on budget items of sizable proportions recommended by an operating vice president for the purchase or rental of a computer to solve technical operating problems. Besides, there is the likelihood that if part of his staff is already servicing the various departments with tabulating and other office equipment, a similar arrangement may be found desirable with electronic machines.

All of this means that if he has already taken a good look at the potential of such equipment, the controller will be in a position to offer a considered opinion when the occasion arises, as well as to take in stride operations which otherwise would be to him totally unfamiliar.

Despite the inevitability of their involvement sooner or later, some companies, for the time being at least, have elected to play an out-waiting game with electronics. By remaining on tried and familiar territory while other companies pioneer, these concerns probably expect that by this means they will gain in the end without having had to traverse the wagon trail of their competitors. However much validity this outlook has, it ignores the value of early know-how gained by firms which collaborate with the appropriate technicians in developing applications. There is also no better means than this to train a nucleus of employees in the special methodology of electronics. In any event, somewhere between complete aloofness and headlong decision lies the desirable middle ground.

And this middle ground governs the course followed in the plan for action. The plan consists of six phases:

1. Establishing clear-cut goals for the program.
2. Organizing properly so that the objectives may be readily achieved.
3. Gathering all the facts that bear on the subject.
4. Developing electronic applications for immediate or future action.
5. Testing the applications.
6. Installing new equipment and procedures if they are warranted by the situation.

No one of the six phases carries a greater import than any other. Together they form a simple common-sense pattern which any controller may easily adapt to his own company's individuality.

Starting with the first phase, consider the goals of the program, or essentially what the controller needs to know. He must determine (a) whether or not his company should buy or rent electronic computing equipment; (b) if it should, which machine or machines should be selected; and (c) once the equipment has been chosen, which of many alternative plans should be followed in its use. These are the three basic objectives.

Once the goals are set, the second phase of the program is the consideration of who is to be responsible for carrying it out. While the controller may provide the leadership, he will, of course, rely heavily on advice and assistance from others in his company, for only through across-the-board co-operation will the desired results be achieved. If he considers his role primarily as that of co-ordinator rather than that of director, the controller is more likely to obtain a generous response when, in search of information, he crosses ever-sacred departmental lines. Of primary importance is the assignment of a full-time co-ordinator — a person possessed of a high-caliber imagination who must be relieved of other duties for as long as is necessary.

Next comes the fact-gathering — the third phase. The controller will at this time want to make the program known to key people in the company. The skill with which he broaches the plan will in no small measure account for its eventual success. Once the plan is understood in all quarters and general enthusiasm has been aroused, the spadework may begin in earnest.

The fact-gathering breaks down into four areas of research: (a) the concept of electronic data processing and the techniques which are used, (b) the equipment itself and what it will and will not do, (c) proven and planned applications of other companies, and (d) procedures and computations which the company making the study believes might be accomplished better electronically.

Since a first concern is with underlying principles, the co-ordinator will wish to familiarize himself with the growing body of not-too-technical literature in this field. He also has available a variety of technical and semitechnical courses of varying duration, which educational institutions and some of the manufacturers of equipment provide for just this purpose. At the same time, he will be exploring the second area of interest from which he will learn the attributes and limitations of machines on the market and on the drawing board as well. From this information there should evolve an inventory of the various items of equipment and their significant characteristics.

After this type of information has been gathered, it is time to turn to the experience of other companies where in many cases it will be found that similar programs have been followed.

The final step in the fact-gathering phase is the preparation of a descriptive listing of all major procedures performed throughout the company, either as part of the flow of work through the office or as separate technical problems. Moreover, technical departments should be canvassed to uncover problems which are not being solved currently because present data-processing methods are too cumbersome. Here is where the controller must call for the active assistance of the operating people. Of course, the analysis of the facts is accompanied by a cost comparison of the present way of doing things and by electronic methods.

On completion of these aspects of fact-finding, the fourth or developmental phase begins. How long after the start of the program this point will arrive depends to a large extent on the variety of company activities that must be reviewed. If the study is to be thorough, the fact-finding should not be rushed. However, the development of conclusions should not be difficult in the light of the completeness of the facts which are at hand at this time.

It may well be that the cost of changing systems will at once indicate that the present is not the appropriate moment to switch from manual to electronic methods. If this be the situation, the program may be readily called off. Should the situation be reversed, and should costs and other pertinent considerations point up appreciable savings or operational improvements by the use of an electronic computer, the selected applications may then be adapted for electronic processing on the appropriate machine. Because of the technical requirements surrounding the way in which information is introduced into the computer, the company which lacks procedure manuals or comparable instructions covering the present way things are done will find it inordinately difficult to convert to electronics.

Beyond the point at which conclusions are reached for the first time, however, there is one further pursuit which the alert controller will follow, regardless of whether or not he identifies potential applications. That pursuit is an outgrowth of the fact-gathering and analysis which have gone before. This body of material may be set down and arranged in the form of a blueprint for the future. Added to and otherwise expanded in detail, the blueprint will plot how all accounting, clerical, and related activities would be carried on *if at some future date a fully electronic office should prove practical for the company.*

The blueprint, which assumes the scrapping of preconceived notions, should de-emphasize costs, since it is inevitable that before too long electronic machines will be somewhat more within reach pricewise than they now are. Even if the blueprint is just tucked away, there will come a time when the controller will be glad he developed it. Central data-processing offices may not be too far away. With continued industrial growth small companies are becoming larger, and what looks impractical today may be an acceptable answer tomorrow. Nor should the controller feel that research of this kind compromises his well-earned reputation for conservatism. The blueprint is nothing more than insurance against a present unknown and a future certainty.

There are basic policies which will influence a company's blueprint. The policy of decentralization is one vivid example. The trend during the past decade has been for American business and industry to decentralize operations to multiple offices. Under this policy the reins have been slackened without a lessening of over-all control as the need for decision-making flexibility has become accentuated. As we all know, it was an uphill fight and in some instances authority was at first delegated grudgingly and sparingly. Then, just as things appeared ready to simmer down, along came the electronic era raising the question: Are we now to scrap it all in favor of centralizing once more? Only if the processing of data is concentrated does the payout of electronics look attractive.

Relatively small and reasonably priced equipment is bound to be developed to do many jobs. However, if there should be a decided advantage in the use of larger and higher-price computers, the principles of decentralization will not be harmed provided the establishment of data-processing centers is considered for those clerical functions that are conducive to centralization without disturbing existing decentralized management. This over-all policy is one of the first considerations that will confront the controller in his preparation of the blueprint of future possibilities in the use of electronics.

So far we have reviewed four of the six phases of the controller's program for action. The last two phases — testing and installation — require little elaboration. Applications selected for the computer should, of course, be thoroughly tested prior to installation. The computer should also be installed with care lest a last-minute slip-up impugn the new method. A subsequent follow-up to make certain that all is well is also an essential.

One final word of caution to controllers who choose to embark on an electronics program is in order. There are many surprises ahead. Equipment for which a company may pay $1 million today may be supplanted tomorrow with a better model costing half as much. Moreover, intricate calculations for which an expensive machine has been bought may become entirely unnecessary as business conditions change. But if these or other heartbreaking things happen, the controller should be of good cheer, because his competitors will find themselves in an identical situation.

Conclusion

By Robert N. Anthony

The purposes for which electronic data-processing equipment will be used in the office can be summarized into three categories.

First, electronic equipment will be used to accomplish *less expensively* jobs that are now being handled manually or by non-electronic equipment. There are machines already in existence, and there are others soon to be available, that can do this in a great many situations.

Second, electronic equipment will be used to produce results *more rapidly* than is possible with existing equipment. The discussion in this chapter seems to indicate that mere speed is not, by itself, likely to be a compelling reason for adopting the new equipment, but rather is in the nature of a corollary advantage — this, despite all the talk about the tremendous speeds at which the new equipment will function.

Third, electronic equipment will be used to provide management with *better information* than it now has. So far we have only a glimpse of the tremendous possibilities that exist for improving the information used for management decisions.

In the short space of time that General Electric has had Univac, management has already discovered that it can be provided information that was not considered obtainable only a couple of years ago because of the limitations of human methods of collecting and analyzing data. As new machines are developed and put into use, our current and necessarily vague idea of the possibilities will, in the near future, give way to demonstrated fact. The "revolution" to which Mr. Osborn refers is upon us, and it will be a stimulating and exciting period.

EFFECTIVE DELEGATION AND CONTROL IN FINANCIAL INSTITUTIONS

Introduction

*By George E. Bates**

In this chapter we are shifting from a *functional* to an *institutional* attack on the problems of delegation and control. One reason is that strictly financial departments (as separate from the controller's department) are rare in all but the largest companies, and so there is not likely to be much "delegation" by the executive responsible for finance in the average manufacturing or mercantile company. Another reason is that in a very real sense the basic elements involved in delegation and control defy segregation on such functional lines.

I think everyone recognizes that what we shall be describing is essentially an "art" — one of the central arts in getting desired action through people. In describing an art, however, we are always in danger of failing to put the flesh and blood of "how to do it in a specific situation" onto the bare bones of a general statement of principle. For this reason we are going to try something of a "case approach." Each author has been asked to describe the way in which he has delegated tasks and controlled resulting actions in his own organization.

* Mr. Bates, who served as moderator for the panel session on which this chapter is based, is James R. Williston Professor of Investment Management, Harvard Business School.

An Investment Banking Organization

*By George D. Woods**

Effective delegation and control must vary with types of business and types of endeavor. The First Boston Corporation, as is true of the other two financial institutions discussed in this chapter, is a service organization. We do not produce anything. We do not process essential raw materials, or fabricate them into some intermediate state, or bring them to the final stage where they are ready for the consumer. The essence of our operation is that The First Boston Corporation — a firm more or less typical of all investment bankers — acts as a conduit between those who require capital and those who have surplus funds.

Our business is concerned primarily with the creation of original issues of securities — the underwriting, the syndicating, and the bringing about of the initial distribution. Another phase of our business is advisory in matters relating to the finances of corporations, municipalities, and other issuers of securities, as well as the direct placement of original issues, as agent, with investors. A third phase is the buying, selling, and trading in outstanding issues of securities, which we do both as broker and as principal. And a fourth phase is, of course, investing for our own account.

That is the business of The First Boston Corporation. We are owned by about 7,000 stockholders, but we endeavor to run the business just as though it were a partnership, because a service organization must be run as a rather personal business.

We delegate responsibility and authority in our firm to the maximum extent. While I am not sure about the accuracy of the figures, I like to think that 50 or 60 per cent of the people in The First Boston Corporation are producing profit and the remainder are the "backer-uppers" — the accountants, the clerical staff, and the

* Mr. Woods is Chairman of the Board, The First Boston Corporation. He has been with this firm since 1934, first as a vice president and director, later as chairman of the executive committee, and for the last three years in his present position.

other employees necessary to support the activities of the producers. A large proportion of that 50 to 60 per cent of our personnel are experts in their own particular lines of endeavor in the investment security business.

At the top of the organization is the executive committee, which might be likened to the partners. Our executive committee consists of nine members, all full-time employees. It of course operates under the authority of a board of directors duly elected by the stockholders. Parenthetically, two-thirds of the members of our board of directors are also full-time employees, with only one-third being "outside" directors.

Our executive committee meets twice a week and specifically authorizes the amount of each new underwriting commitment which our officers may take. The committee goes very little beyond that. It leaves to the officers in charge of our municipal or our corporation buying department complete discretion as to the price and compensation that they will either negotiate or bid. Our top-level executives and the executive committee could not possibly run our business except on the basis of delegating to the knowledgeable people in the government department, the municipal department, the corporation department, full authority to fix prices and compensation. Our executive committee also, in a broad way, authorizes each undertaking we assume with respect to advisory or direct placement services for an issuer.

The executive committee likewise sets the aggregate dollar limits within which the managers of the various units in our trading department may buy and sell for our own account. We have a limitation on what we can have in our portfolio with respect to United States Government securities. We have a limit on the number of acceptances, a limit on corporation bonds and stocks, a limit on the amount of bank and insurance stocks, and a limit on the amount of obligations of municipalities or other political subdivisions — both United States and Canadian — which our trading department may own. However, the executive committee delegates to the managers of the various types of trading activity full authority with respect to price. The only limitation is that of aggregate quantities.

The basic limitation on capital employed in the various departments and divisions is net worth. Clearly the aggregate of all the authorizations in various lines of trading activity plus the current volume of the new issue underwriting business plus our own investment portfolio must have a reasonable relationship to our net worth. To illustrate:

We find that in order to be a factor in the United States Government bond business the limitations have to be extremely large. Our current authorizations — we are trading in the three general categories of government bonds, i.e., short, medium, and long-term — are more than $400 million. At the other extreme, we find that in the bank and insurance stock business our authorizations can be relatively small — perhaps a half a million dollars.

We have found, by a cut-and-try experience over 20 years, about what is needed to be a factor in the different categories of securities. The justification for periodically increasing or decreasing certain lines is the feeling that any of us on the executive committee level may have about interest rates or stock market possibilities in general. If we feel that things are a little strained, we do not tell our corporate bond trader to sell this or that or the other bond, but we tell him to decrease his position and to be at the desired point in 30 days.

In general, the basic determinant is the amount of our capital. Subsidiary to that is our experience regarding the size of an authorization that a manager has to have to be a factor in his area of activity. And on those two bases, every three or six months we review the issues and apply our judgment in the light of the then current situation.

Our executive committee studies with great care each new investment which we propose to make for our own account. In our business, dealing entirely in investment securities, our stock in trade is our trading portfolio. Every now and then we make an investment for our own account. Implicit in such an investment is the intention that we will hold the item for a minimum of six months, so that, in the event of a sale at a profit, we realize a capital gain. It is by law rather than by policy that the making of such special investments is under the supervision of a group other than the normal day-to-day managers of our business. Therefore decisions relating to an investment for our own account are reserved to the executive committee, and are not delegated.

Outside of that, our officers and employees at the various levels and in the various departments are almost completely on their own with respect to what they do within policy limitations. This way of operating is a necessity because in our business the activity varies. Every day we have hundreds of individual purchases and sales, and on many days there are thousands. On a day when the actual syndication of a new issue of securities takes place, we have had more than 10,000 separate transactions. So each of our people has to make up his own mind on the basis of the facts of life — and of the markets — as he sees them at the time.

I agree with General Clay (see Part I) that the matter of delegation is an art. The matter of control, of course, is more of a science. We have no organization chart in The First Boston Corporation, except in our accounting division. We have a pretty close organization chart in this division where we keep score on the performance of our seven offices and our various departments or groups that trade and deal in different types of securities.

Outside of this score-keeping activity, the principal control in the operation of our security business is the profit motive. Each one of our people is conscious of the fact that while he receives a specified annual compensation, this may be increased substantially, depending on the over-all profit of the corporation but more particularly on his own performance. The more mistakes in judgment he makes, the less satisfying his business performance will look at the end of the year. These performance figures are reviewed semi-annually.

Other than these performance figures, we have in our office what we have come to call the 30-day list, which in a way also goes to the profit matter or motive. Dealing in securities which invariably we buy for the purpose of reselling at a profit, those of us on the executive committee level exhibit a rather deep curiosity about anything we have in our regular trading (as distinguished from our investment) portfolio for as long as 30 days. I no longer have to go down the list of securities on the left-hand side to look at the date acquired; I can merely go down the right-hand side and compare the purchase and current market prices. If the current market price is below our cost, the chances are that we have owned the item longer than would normally be the case—most security traders hate to take a loss. We carefully watch when our activity in day-to-day business results in carrying securities in our portfolio for longer than 30 days and, failing a good reason, we instruct that they be sold when this point has been reached. That is the principal method of control as far as day-to-day trading business is concerned.

We have another general rule, and that is with respect to original issues of securities. If we have any unsold balances of original issues of securities at the end of 10 full business days after the initial offering, we examine the reasons. If there has been a change in the market or if the judgment our officers exercised in fixing the original offering price was faulty, we take such action as may be indicated in the light of the facts.

In this area of delegation and control, the most important thing, as I have just described, is to give full authority to our officers and department managers with respect to the price they will pay and the price at which they will sell. The most difficult thing is to take a loss. Experience has taught me that, generally speaking, the first loss is the best loss. A going business must keep capital flowing. It should not turn itself into a conduit so clogged that it cannot continue to take new commitments.

Effective delegation of authority must be built, in the final analysis, on the bringing along of younger men in an organization—finding young men, training them, bringing them up to a point, and then seeing how they perform when they are thrown into the cold water—taking responsibility.

It takes trainees about a year and a half to go through the various departments in our organization to see what the investment security business is all about. A total of three years is needed for training in most activities and a somewhat longer period for preparation for the buying end of the business. For instance, it takes from five to seven years to accumulate the background needed to work on original issues of securities. There should be a maximum amount of time and patience in the matter of education—and a period of watchful waiting to get some of the theories into practice.

I know of no criteria, and I cannot imagine any, for deciding when a young man is ready for responsibility. A trainee gets to the point where he should be thrown into the cold water and left to sink or make the shore when the administrator responsible for throwing him in has that hunch. And, of course, that hunch is a gamble.

If this cold-water concept sounds extreme, let me point out that first we try to teach the would-be cold-water enthusiast how to swim, leading him into deeper and deeper water. And of course we give different people different degrees of responsibility at different rates. But at the same time there is a limit to the amount of time and patience in this matter of education. There is some point at which the trainee must be in the cold water by himself.

If a young man is at a trading desk, buying and selling bonds, and the chief trader is on his vacation, and the two top assistants are away because one of them is having a baby and the other one has a broken leg, and a call comes in, "I want a bid for two million" — well, right there and then, our young man is in the cold water. (Or it may be the hot water!) At some point the officer who happens to be running that end of the business has got to say to himself, "I am going to absent myself and see what happens."

We try to take on a minimum of six or seven young men a year. Our experience since 1946 has been that about one-third of these men will leave in the course of the first two years, and another third will leave within five years. But we keep one-third, and we have to be satisfied with that record. I have noticed that the third which stays with us are seriously interested in the business, have a sense of urgency about it, and are willing to accept responsibility. They make mistakes, but rarely if ever make the same mistake twice.

Another plus, from our point of view, is that many of those who leave us go to other security firms where they think the prospects are better. Almost invariably this change means we have a friend in another smaller security firm — sometimes a more specialized business. The First Boston Corporation has a great many graduates in the security field.

The matter of bringing men along in the organization leads to a related problem: whether contacts established by older members of the organization can be passed along to younger members so that a continuing relationship will exist should the older member die or retire. Broadly speaking, there are two aspects to our business. As I said at the outset, we are a conduit. And a conduit has business at both ends.

As far as that end of the business which has to do with the origination of securities is concerned, we are dealing with corporate officers, or appointed or elected officers of political entities. It is very much the exception rather than the rule for only one person to engage in such dealings. By their very nature three or four people are involved, and there is no problem in bringing young men into these discussions. The terms and conditions of the contract form one aspect; the preparation of selling literature is another aspect; the investigating of the engineering and business phases form still another aspect; and finally there are the negotiations relating to price.

As far as the other side of the conduit is concerned—the end that has to do with those who have surplus funds—it seems to me that this is rather more of a personalized business. Whether we are talking of individuals or trustees, a man develops confidence in the judgment of a certain security dealer, just as he develops confidence in an accountant or an engineer or a doctor. As to those individuals—the private investors—there has not yet been devised any completely satisfactory way of passing that business relationship along from the older to the younger generation.

However, a most important facet of that end of our business has to do with professional or institutional investors. When doing business with any well-organized institutional investor, the security dealer has two or three men carrying on the discussions. The professional investor knows about markets and proper pricing. He might want to hear some discussion to clarify or crystallize his own thinking, but he is not particularly interested in hearing arguments on price. On the other hand he is very much interested in getting the statistical facts and the economic background of the industry involved, the facts relating to the issuer and the specific security under consideration. And he quite often gets into legal questions. So there are always two or three people who deal with the large professionals, and again in this area of our activity there is no unusual problem in bringing along the young men — from whom will be developed the future members of our executive committee — and having them observe and learn.

In a Commercial Bank

*By Nathaniel M. Symonds**

Before we can discuss any problems involved in delegation and the controls used to support it, we need to know, of course, the nature of the work being delegated.

This section concerns a commercial bank. Probably all of you are familiar to a degree with the objectives of the commercial banking business, over and above that of making a profit for the stockholders; in other words, those objectives which create the need for delegation of responsibility. Reduced to simplest terms, the banking department of a commercial bank is interested in obtaining deposits and putting those deposits to work to produce interest earnings; the trust department administers property for the benefit of others at a fee; the bond department, as principal or agent, deals in the purchase and sale of permitted bonds; the service and staff departments facilitate the operation of the income producing departments.

We must remember, of course, that a bank exists for its customers. Perhaps this should be the first objective described, since it is of primary importance. Thus, we could state the objectives of the commercial banking business from the point of view of the customer: a place for individuals or corporations to deposit funds or secure loans of a temporary nature; a permanent organization to

* Mr. Symonds is Vice President, The Northern Trust Company, Chicago. Mr. Symonds has been with this bank for 25 years. In 1946 he became a vice president and now is senior vice president in the commercial banking department.

act as trustee; a source from which to purchase investments of United States Government, state, or municipal bonds; or, in general, an institution supplying financial services. Clearly, the objectives illustrate the need for delegation.

There is another set of circumstances to bear in mind, however—namely, the kind of bank under discussion. We are a "unit bank," if for no other reason than that the constitution of the State of Illinois, under which we operate, does not permit branch banking. We offer from only one location a variety of financial services to corporations and to individuals.

Another characteristic of the bank lies in the nature of the business which we now serve and which we seek to serve. As a large bank, the services offered are to individuals mainly in the average to above-average income brackets and to corporate customers having above-average net worth. These objectives are understandable because the single location of the bank in the central part of Chicago is not conducive to the supplying of financial services to the broad mass of people all over the city (though we do have many thousands of customers, and we do have small accounts).

With this description, a comparatively simple interior organization might be expected. The normal stockholder-director responsibility is, of course, present. Executive responsibility rests with the president and is administered through two executive vice presidents and the department heads. The directors meet monthly, and an executive committee of the board of directors meets weekly.

Because I share the responsibility for the banking department, and also because the organization here is typical, I will enlarge on its particular structure:

Six divisions take care of commercial business, one division takes care of personal accounts, one the foreign business, one the savings business, and one the service functions. Each of these ten divisions generally is headed by a vice president, and various other officers are included on the division staff.

The commercial divisions are responsible for customers and prospects in certain industry classifications within the City of Chicago and all business and prospects in certain geographical areas.

Three divisions cover geographical responsibilities: one division handles everything west of the Mississippi River; one the states of Illinois, Michigan, and Wisconsin; and a third everything east of the Mississippi River except those three states. Within the cities of Chicago and New York the industry classifications prevail.

To the extent of the geographical arrangement, overlapping of responsibilities is not a problem, but in Chicago and New York it is possible to have several vice presidents of the bank in the city at one time. In doing the work of the bank in a city of such size, this situation is to be expected. But there is no conflict as far as the assignments are concerned, because within those two cities the assignments are on an industry basis. It is true that the individual officers of the bank are brought into conversations and discussions on many problems that are outside their particular responsibility. But ultimately the responsibility comes back to the assigned source.

In the delegated responsibility of each of the divisions you will find nearly all banking operations performed, and in a sense each division is a bank unto itself. Actually the responsibilities that each division head carries are as great as in many banks in the country. In this respect is found another of the characteristics of the business: the need for a relatively large proportion of officers to total employees.

This organization and resulting delegation brings at once the problems of controlling performance with respect to the servicing, credit, business development responsibilities, expenses, personnel needs, and, in general, adherence to policies issued at the executive or department level. With this description of the organization, the theory and problem of delegation with us become understandable.

Institutional policy flows from the president through the executive vice presidents to the departments, and within the departments to the divisions. Likewise, departmental policy flows to the divisions from the vice presidents in charge. The transmission of such policies may be oral or written. Institutional matters may take the form of published executive instructions, and likewise departmental matters may be issued as departmental instructions. Matters of lesser consequence resulting from day-to-day discussion and routine activity may be passed by memoranda or by word of mouth.

I could of course comment extensively on that side of the banking business which is precise. But, since we are focusing our attention on the broader problems in delegation, I shall not dwell on those problems that are involved in accounting procedures and operating practices, or legal restrictions, or those that involve relations with banking authorities (the Federal Reserve or the state officials). Obviously such problems are dealt with daily; and in all of these delegations of responsibility are involved, but I believe I can better indicate some of the problems of delegation in the business in broader terms. For example:

> An illustration of delegated responsibility is the authority given to divisional officers to grant loans. This responsibility is delegated by executive instructions or, in other words, prescribed by the president. These instructions state in detail the dollar limits within which each officer is authorized to make various types of loans. They are developed by the senior banking officers with assistance from the division heads, and as they are formulated within the department they are submitted to the president with recommendation for final adoption. Once accepted and issued to all officers involved, these executive instructions establish authorities and responsibilities which rest with the individual in the department.

In this illustration one point should be made particularly clear. Although the limits of authorities are stated in detail, the limitation is increased where *two* officers join in the credit extension. The point here to note is the importance of communication between the officers.

The commercial banking business is such that many of its dealings are in areas where there are no clear-cut patterns. The deposit and earning assets vary in size and quality, changing from time to time and calling for continuing judgment regarding the character and credit worthiness of the customer, the term of the loan, the interest rate, the repayment, and many other factors. The proper handling of all these factors involves almost a continuing discussion, not only between the officer of the bank handling the account and the customer, but also between the officer and his associates.

Then there is the matter of solicitation of new business by the banking department and its referral of such business to the trust department. The banking and investment officers, for instance, are, by the nature of the business, more active within the community and within the geographical territories which they cover than are our trust officers. They also have opportunities for talking business with other departments of the bank. The effective use of these banking department officers comes through a system of education of the men and the department to the potentials of the business.

So far as our commercial business is concerned, we get the corporate trustee appointments that would normally result from such activity. Any enlargement of this business, though, depends on the way we handle the individual business that exists.

Since our institution is a unit bank, we do not have exposure to our individual customers to the same degree that those banks which operate branches do. We recognize that disadvantage, and we have formed a division of the banking department which deals solely with the personal business that is both on our books and in prospect. The function of those in this division throughout the day, the week, the month, the year, is not only seeing our personal customers, but seeking every possibility for service to them from all departments of the bank.

This division is made up of five officers and the secretary, hand-picked for the personal business; and it includes people who have been trust officers, commercial banking officers, and service officers of the bank, and, incidentally, one of them has had experience in the bond department. The variety gives us every possible exposure to the three major income-producing departments of the bank which can be applied to the solicitation of personal business.

To a degree, then, we find in the nature of the business that delegation and control go almost hand in hand. We have delegated to a division the responsibility for the development of business, and this in turn has been delegated within the division to an officer. With the development may come not only the securing of the deposit relationship but potentially the extension of credit. As business is solicited, the divisional associates of the officer are kept informed of the calls that are made, the problems of securing a foothold in the financial affairs of the company, and, assuming success in the first instance, the conferences with the customer to discuss credit needs. Such discussions frequently involve two or more of the officers of the division, and whether or not the business is consummated, the proper record is made for the files of all the circumstances involved.

Much of this control, which is in reality keeping associates informed rather than the routine control of action, comes through the series of meetings for which banks are so noted. Actually, delegation flows through the organization to the point where a great deal of the bank's business is decided on and accomplished at the level of immediate contact between the officer and customer. And, since delegation flows from the top, the control or communication starts at the bottom. To summarize:

(1) We have communication between the officers, which ultimately ends up in a weekly divisional meeting to review all activity of the division including loans, servicing problems, and new business efforts.

(2) The next step up in reporting or control lies in the departmental meetings. These, likewise, are held periodically. Those of a credit nature — in other words, these discussions that are concerned with the department's earning assets — are held weekly; new business matters are considered monthly; and servicing problems are taken up at the weekly meeting of the cashier's division.

(3) From the department such matters are carried to a weekly meeting of the senior banking officers with the president, held prior to the formal presentation to the executive committee of the board.

On a broader approach, control also is exercised by means of formal periodic reports. Each division prepares such a report quarterly, and the division reports are subsequently summarized in a department report. All these reports are directed to the president, and they cover in detail matters relating to deposits, loans, interest rates, business development activity, personnel, and expenses.

Obviously, the success of such a practice of delegation and control depends ultimately on the caliber of the people involved. Whether the delegation is written or oral, the principles of brevity, clarity, and simplicity are important. We try to give perspective along with the delegation; and we support the delegation with the necessary authority. We provide in the service and staff departments of the bank the technical knowledge needed to carry out an assignment.

In our controls we try to be natural rather than restrictive. In any endeavor there is an understandable pride of accomplishment which encourages communication. Where there has been no accomplishment, or where it has been to a somewhat lesser degree than hoped for — which would perhaps discourage communication — we analyze the reason first at the divisional level. We use the example to stimulate confidence and to secure direction and additional assistance needed. All of this creates understanding between people who work closely together as an entire organization, and whose work is the basis of the resulting reputation of the bank. Therefore, we want to be very sure of the people to whom we are delegating responsibilities.

We work toward an adequate number of trained people on our staff and an adequate number of people in training who will provide the replacements for the staff. We must be sure that these people are motivated to accept delegation, assume responsibility, and participate in the controls. The development of men along these lines lessens the need for restrictive techniques of delegation and control.

In conclusion, the problems of effective delegation and control, as we experience them, are to a large extent centered in communications, which is certainly a more intangible and perhaps an even more difficult subject than that of delegation and control. Words have different meanings for different people. If we are sure our words are understood as we delegate, the value of rigid controls beyond the exact phases of the business is questionable.

In an Insurance Organization

*By William S. Youngman, Jr.**

Only five years ago, I moved from one profession — the law — to what has become another profession — business.

* Mr. Youngman is President, C. V. Starr & Company, Inc.; Chairman of the Board, Globe and Rutgers Fire Insurance Company, American Home Assurance Company, Insurance Company of the State of Pennsylvania; Director, American International Underwriters Corporation. Until five years ago Mr. Youngman practiced law, beginning his career in 1932 with a one-year appointment as secretary

When I undertook my present job, as chief executive officer of a relatively large world-wide insurance organization employing several thousand people, the founder of the business told me that if I organized my work well and delegated it properly, he would not care whether I worked more than a few hours a month or where in the world I worked. While I cannot presume to have achieved the optimum of the founder, the philosophy of very complete delegation prevails in our organization.

My education in the "art of delegation" began as the manager of a football team more than 25 years ago. I remember that we were then confronted with very simple problems compared to what we have now. If the vice president in charge of the weather was doubtful of the clouds on the day of the game, we frequently had to change a great many cleats in the few minutes before the kickoff. We solved that problem by delegating it to the players themselves and later by providing them with two pairs of shoes.

However, I face now as I did then the problems of (a) an assistant being given too much or too little to do, and (b) the staff member not well suited to his task. In addition, I now have somewhat more refined problems, such as how to make a good business manager sales-minded or a good salesman an orderly administrator, or how to supplement one with the other.

To use Mr. Bates's phrase, how can one deal with the problem of "getting desired action through people"? Clearly there must be the following elements, among others:

1. Decentralization.
2. Division of the problem into units.
3. Delegation of responsibility and the authority necessary to carry it out.
4. Proper selection and placement of the best available personnel — an understanding of their personalities and abilities.
5. Imaginative leadership with occasionally at least a dash of inspiration.
6. A policy of keeping hands off even at times when mistakes may be made.

---

to Judge Learned Hand. His subsequent legal experience was in private practice and in government service, where he was chief counsel and general counsel for several agencies and commissions, including the Federal Power Commission.

I remember a story told about Marshal Foch. Someone visited his headquarters and found him reading a book at the height of a battle. On inquiry, it developed that the Marshal had given orders that if his troops advanced beyond a certain point or fell back behind a certain point, he was to be notified; otherwise, he was not to be disturbed.

Our business, by its very nature, requires extensive delegation. Since our senior company is primarily a holding and advisory concern, matters of management are automatically delegated to subsidiaries or affiliates. If the officers of the senior company find themselves getting into direct management, someone is usually not doing a good job, perhaps because of ineffective delegation.

The operations break down into four separate organizations or groups of operating companies with completely separate personnel and management:

1. General insurance on risks overseas written abroad through a separate subsidiary agency company in each country.
2. Similar overseas risks written in the United States through branches in the principal cities — what is called "home-foreign" business.
3. Domestic fire and marine insurance companies in the United States — for example, Globe and Rutgers Fire Insurance Company and the American Home Assurance Company.
4. Life insurance companies abroad in the Philippines, Hong Kong, Malaya, Venezuela, Cuba, Mexico, and other countries. These companies are sometimes quite large; in the Philippines our company has several thousand employees and full-time agents.

Since we are primarily engaged in overseas business with separate companies in most countries, these organizations, of necessity, are managed locally. Thus we start off with a good measure of corporate and geographic decentralization.

I believe that courageous delegation has been encouraged by the owner-management element in our business. Our number of stockholders is relatively small — about 30 people who are active in the business, and their families. Since we are both managers and owners, there has been a wider range of discretion in developing our business and in delegation than I have observed in most other insurance operations.

The primary function of our senior company is that of representing the stockholders. Accordingly, it concerns itself with:

1. *Top policy.* The executives frequently have to make the difficult decisions about new capital investment — whether to buy a new company in the United States or to increase the capital of a company in a foreign country.
2. *Top personnel.* Our senior company may influence the decision as to who will become a top overseas or regional executive, but most personnel matters are delegated to the operating companies or to their local managers.
3. *Investments.* The senior company has in theory supreme investment authority, but in practice this is largely delegated.
4. *The figures.* The senior company analyzes the figures which are produced in the field as a record of the past and a guide to the future. It watches over and, in a sense, polices the operations through a group of traveling auditors, who operate somewhat as bank examiners do in the United States.

In the United States, executive functions are normally carried out with the aid of our policy committee — a small advisory committee, composed of our senior executives, which meets twice a month. However, executives are urged to carry out fully the functions of their offices, make decisions on their own, and merely report the results to the committee — even to the extent of making mistakes sometimes.

By advising or consulting our policy committee regarding important matters of policy we keep our key personnel informed, which is essential to good management and wise delegation.

I know of some large companies that are run by committees with a unanimous vote necessary for action. In our type of organization, however, such a rule would be unnecessarily cumbersome and time-consuming. As for not believing in committees, I judge that we are in agreement with the point of view expressed at the Business Conference last year by Ralph Cordiner, President of General Electric.[1]

We try to give our executives wide authority. For example, our treasurer has extensive responsibilities in keeping track of the cash

[1] Edward C. Bursk, Editor, *How to Increase Executive Effectiveness* (Cambridge, Harvard University Press, 1953), pp. 24–31.

position of our operations throughout the world in order to see that we mobilize our cash most effectively. As he has carried out this function, he has found that local companies tend to hold on to more cash than they need for their own operations and to have too many bank accounts, with the result that a great deal of cash may lie idle merely because of lack of organization.

We also have an investment subcommittee which meets infrequently to consider the problems of investment of available funds in several score countries throughout the world. This committee meets infrequently because the investment work is delegated to various experts. Among others, there are two currency experts who deal not only in problems of foreign exchange but also in foreign investment, particularly in parts of the world where the currencies are soft. In such areas it is often necessary to abandon orthodox concepts of what constitutes a "safe" investment and buy equities, land, or other hedges against inflation.

A specialist in investment in the United States is also given wide authority. He advises our domestic fire and marine insurance companies on their bond and stock investments and, subject to the approval of the small finance committee of the boards of directors of these companies, is largely responsible for the management of their portfolios.

This delegation is not as extensive as that described by Boyd Everett, Vice President and Treasurer of the Continental Assurance Company,[2] who had the authority on his own initiative to buy securities for his company, subject to later ratification by the finance committee. However, our procedure is set up to allow speedy action between finance committee meetings after informal consultation.

In the larger, more influential countries abroad there are small investment committees consisting of the local manager or his representative and a local expert. These committees or the individual managers may bring important problems to the officers in the United States for advice.

There is also a small personnel subcommittee, the members of which are constantly studying the personnel problems of our organ-

[2] Edward C. Bursk, Editor, *op. cit.*, pp. 108–116.

ization. This committee meets from time to time and considers the assignment of key people about the world; it tries to spot promising young men, develops standards for overseas personnel, determines suitable training programs, and aids the personnel department in the appraisal of applicants. Nevertheless, the local managers are necessarily given a wide degree of discretion regarding employment, wages, and conditions of work of most of the personnel in their own organizations.

As for the way controls work in our organization, let me turn to our overseas operations, where we have over 70 companies. The local manager of each company has been delegated the highest possible discretion to direct its operations. However, the following controls are retained over each manager:

(1) The local manager must submit an annual budget and quarterly comparisons of actual income and expenditures.

(2) The local manager must file a brief monthly report with figures and comments regarding any new problems or developments.

(3) In addition to the team of traveling accountants previously mentioned, one of whom may appear at any time to audit accounts anywhere in the world, outside auditors are employed as well.

(4) Since the overseas companies are self-contained units, a small group of top American operating executives resident overseas, including some regional executives, travel constantly visiting these companies, appraising the managers, and working with them on their financial and production problems.

(5) Contrary to the views of many companies that use of the telephone and frequent travel are wasteful, we have a policy encouraging all top executives and local managers to travel — to visit the United States and other offices — and to use the telephone frequently. We have found this most effective in keeping in close touch with overseas offices, and most helpful in improving the morale of everyone, particularly the managers who live abroad.

It is so easy for the foreign local manager to feel abandoned, or out of touch with the United States or the head office. I remember this especially when during the war I was in Chungking, China, surrounded by the Japanese, and we had to code every message sent out of the country and then we had to wait a week or 10 days for the answer. It really does bother one to be so far removed and out of touch.

Delegation is usually so great in overseas operations that our problem is often one of keeping the top executives in the United States and abroad and the overseas managers closely enough in touch with one another. It is most important to make the various parts of the organization feel they are in close communication and understand one another.

The success of operations is largely dependent on the type of local managers obtained in each country and the extent to which operations are delegated to them. We have a well-established policy of selecting a national as manager in each country if this is at all possible. And in 34 years of operation we have never had a case of misplaced trust. The local managers come to know us closely. For instance, they send their children to the United States, and we watch over them in schools here. We would not hesitate to reverse the process where desirable.

Usually almost all the other employees in a local office are also nationals. However, if a particular manager is relatively new to the organization, he is generally provided with a full-time American associate who is familiar with the organization and functions of the business.

It takes an average of seven years to know enough about the business to be an effective overseas manager, even though a manager may have had some domestic experience beforehand. Consequently, we follow a policy of picking people as young as we can. Another reason for so doing is that in the overseas business particularly there are conditions that are hard on a person—for example, there are still parts of the world where the anopheles mosquito is to be encountered.

An insurance organization operating overseas faces many problems: local insurance laws (frequently nationalistic), exchange difficulties, labor problems, relations with the staff, an all-important production problem, and others. Generally speaking, delegation of these problems to good nationals is far more effective than having an outsider deal with them. In addition it is far more economical, since the cost of training and sending an American overseas is very large, and the problems of adjustment frequently difficult for him and his family.

Any medium-size or larger overseas office will also normally have one or more full-time Americans who help in the production of American business and in other ways. These form a group of so-called "overseas personnel" who are handled along similar lines to the foreign-service personnel in our State Department. Among themselves, they have comparable standards of pay, cost-of-living allowances appropriate to their location, and other privileges, as well as job rotation approximately every three years.

In the insurance business there are a number of key figures concerning production and results which if examined systematically give a speedy and effective check on field operations. One of the reasons the founder of the business was so optimistic that far-flung operations could be followed and guided in a minimum amount of time was that he believed that a regular check of key figures plus familiarity with the personality of the managers provided in themselves much of the knowledge necessary for effective delegation and control.

We get from our branch offices and overseas companies flash reports on premium volume, losses, collections, cash, and other items that enable us to keep constantly in touch with the progress or retrogression of the business in a given territory.

The multiplicity of our affairs and operations is such that only by the type of organization I have described are we able to carry on our business efficiently or even carry it on at all.

While we try to achieve a maximum of delegation and a minimum of central control, naturally we have some problems that break through the lines of authority, delegation, and control. Some matters arise that are so important that anyone in the organization who can help must do so, regardless of organizational charts, committees, and the like. However, I have noticed that these problems seem to get fewer as our delegation improves, and our senior executives therefore are given more time for creative thinking and association with others both inside and outside our organization who may have helpful ideas or projects.

Among the joys of delegation in a world-wide organization are the frequent surprises provided by the unexpected successes of an effective local leader or manager. While occasionally we receive bad news from different parts of the world, such as unexpected currency devaluations, nearly every day we learn of some small or large accomplishment that justifies our policy of giving to a man of ability as much scope and freedom of action as possible.

Perhaps I have dwelt at too great length on my own particular business which, because of its complexity, diversity, and broad compass, makes delegation of authority almost unavoidable. It seems to me, however, that the principle of delegation applies not only to such an enterprise as this, but in varying degrees to any business whatever its nature, and that successful delegation of authority is an art which must be studied and learned well if the lives of both the business and the executive are to be long and prosperous.

EFFECTIVE DELEGATION AND CONTROL BY THE SALES EXECUTIVE

In a Textile Operation

*By E. H. Brown**

Let me begin by commenting on a sentence taken from the previous book in this series, *How to Increase Executive Effectiveness:* "Apparently the job descriptions many companies use have little to do with the way the company really operates."[1] How true this is, and of course how wrong it is, but how much more is it true on the particular subject of delegation and control by the sales executive! That point is one I have really considered as I brought together my observations for this chapter.

The typical American business starts as a small, one-man operation — very simple to control and with little need for delegation. Then, as the business grows in size or complexity or both, the need for delegation and control quickly develops. And, as growth continues, more and more companies expand into diversified businesses where the proper balance between delegation and control in all phases of the operation is essential.

That briefly is the story of the Kendall Company with which I am associated. Fifty years ago, ours was a very small, one-man operation in one field of endeavor. Last year, our sales exceeded $100 million. Our business now covers surgical dressings, elastic goods, industrial tapes, textiles, curtain goods, athletic goods, diapers, foot products, and a few others. Some of our merchandise is found in almost every retail outlet in America as well as in hospitals and in

* Mr. Brown is Director of Sales for the Chicago Division of the Kendall Company. He joined the Bauer & Black Division of that company and was assigned as field sales manager in 1942. In 1948 he became general sales manager of Bauer & Black, and in 1954 assumed his present position.

[1] Edward C. Bursk, Editor (Cambridge, Harvard University Press, 1953), p. 68.

industrial plants; and we also do export business. We have 14 plants in the United States and plants in Canada, Mexico, and Cuba.

With this diversification, balanced delegation and control are obviously essential. This means that the biggest job of the sales executive is the selection and development of men. That point is certainly covered very well in the early chapters of this book. This is the beginning and the end of delegation and control. Without this it is impossible.

The basic principle or philosophy of our company is one of decentralization, of operating responsibilities properly coupled with centralized co-ordination and control. Again, those are merely words unless they are interpreted in action.

Having established this broad principle, we have found it advisable and necessary first to prepare an organizational statement and then to carry through with job descriptions, with a management handbook defining divisional authority and responsibility, and with basic statistical and financial reports tied to forecasts and budgets. This gives us definite guideposts — a structure, if you will, to help in understanding and accomplishing delegation and control. It is of course constantly necessary to keep these guideposts moving as the company moves and as men within the company move.

At Bauer & Black and throughout the Kendall Company we have operated to build our management organization rather than to attempt to obtain management from the outside. There are some penalties for this, but we believe the advantages outweigh the penalties. So much in the understanding and appreciation of company principles, philosophies, or objectives, call them what you will, cannot be instilled or accomplished in a conversation but rather requires broad experience and development within the company.

Our experience I believe has not been unlike that of many growing American companies in the need and desire to improve our position constantly as regards effective sales delegation and control. We usually start that improvement when we run into problems rather than before we run into them. I would like to say we start it first, but, to be completely honest, we usually try to improve after we see trouble brewing.

The Bauer & Black Division started with surgical dressings, elastic goods, and foot products. They were our basic businesses 25 years ago. As we grew, we started an industrial tape business, an athletic goods business, and an export business. Each of these and the three original businesses grew substantially, and we found ourselves with sales management in the hands of men with broad experience in the original businesses but limited experience in the new businesses. Naturally this led to a feeling of neglect on the part of the new, fast-growing businesses. They felt like stepchildren, but, more important, there was a tendency to do too much delegation and too little control in some places and too little delegation and too much control in other places. Human beings, even executives, tend to want to do a lot of the things they feel they do well and know the most about.

This situation led in the last year and a half to the establishment of the Chicago Division of the Kendall Company in an attempt to solve the problem of delegation and control. The division is made up of a divisional manager, a director of sales, a director of production, and a controller; this group is known as the Chicago executive organization. A general sales manager was established as the major executive for each of our businesses. Biweekly or weekly, depending on the size of the business involved, we have scheduled conferences between the general sales manager of each business and the Chicago executive organization. The general sales manager prepares an agenda in advance subject to any additions members of the Chicago executive organization may want to make.

This regular contact supplies, we believe, necessary control with maximum delegation. The meetings provide orderly and systematic interchange of information and assist executives in the solution of their problems but do not overstep the principles of delegation.

Of course, the meetings are supplemented by individual contacts and by established statistical or control reports. I share the conviction that personal contacts are important but also believe that really effective personal contacts require a substantial background of information which can come only from statistical facts. Yet one cannot blindly accept conclusions reached from statistical data any more than he can blindly accept the personal contact technique. Herein lies the opportunity for the best in sales management — to reach a strong middle ground using all the tools available.

(The reader may well ask: With delegation a prime objective, what need is there for any centralized sales organization in a company like Kendall where there are autonomous operating divisions manufacturing diversified products? Part of the answer is that in our various businesses there are conflicting channels of distribution. For example, we produce athletic supporters. One of our divisions sells them in the drug field. Another division sells them in the sporting goods field. There is a real job in co-ordinating plans, co-ordinating pricing, taking care of potential or actual distribution mixups. The second part of the answer is that we are customers of one another's divisions, and the central group has an important part in keeping the seller-buyer relationship straight within the company.)

Our individual sales departments are organized with a general sales manager at the top, then a field sales manager, branch managers, and district managers. The major delegation of broad responsibilities is at the branch level — for hiring men, for compensation recommendations, for development of men, and of course for business getting, branch budgets, sales expense, and sales forecasts. Unless the field sales manager is constantly working with the branch manager on basic sales standards, calls, orders, coverage, and expense, the variation becomes tremendous because of too much delegation and too little control. Extremes quickly develop: the one extreme, too much control so that the objective is lost; the other, no control with complete delegation to the salesman. The main purpose at field management meetings is to work constantly to keep the proper balance.

Some 25 years ago I had a personal experience on the subject of too much and too little delegation that made a very real impression on me. It was, I believe, the subject reduced to its simplest form:

I was at the time assigned to the sales-operating part of our business where we studied sales coverage, potentials, calls, and so on. One of our experienced, seasoned sales managers came down to discuss several matters relative to his branch with us, and in the course of the conversation he mentioned one of his men. I took advantage of this opening to expose my knowledge and proceeded to lay out all the facts and statistics which indicated what was wrong with this man — calls, coverage, routing, reports — everything. The sales manager waited patiently until I finished my exposé and then said, "Yes, you know, Ed, the only thing that blankety-blank so-and-so can do is sell." There was quite a pause while I absorbed my lesson.

Of course both of us were in error. I was attempting to form a conclusion based only on statistical data. He, on the other hand, was using as a control only sales dollars. Time showed both of us wrong. That is where we have erred in the past, probably will err in the future — in not accomplishing the proper balance. That is where most companies err, and to correct that error is the objective we are all reaching for in management.

Two paragraphs in *Executive Action* contain much meat for us and are important both in the handling of our regular meetings and whenever contacts are made in between the meetings.[2] The first deals with a Mr. Wood who is depicted as the executive accomplishing successful delegation: "He had realized, between his 45th and 50th years, that the satisfaction of letting other men learn often outweighed, in the long run, the satisfaction of doing things himself." And later from the section "Control and Measurement": "The principal contribution which top executives make to the control process is through the attitudes they express . . ."

To illustrate the importance of these two points, here is another incident from my own experience:

I attended a sales conference of one of our businesses. The merchandising manager in presenting his plans, his programs, and his products moved from that part of his job which was his job to the details, then to instructions to the salesmen on how to do their jobs. Sitting in the audience I could easily see how rapidly he lost his salesmen. He lost them completely. He lost them because he was failing to delegate responsibility for that great ability that salesmen have — creative selling. He was not satisfied to do his job on merchandising and planning and

[2] Edmund P. Learned, David N. Ulrich, and Donald R. Booz, *Executive Action* (Boston, Division of Research, Harvard Business School, 1951), pp. 96, 136.

products, but he carried on through to the details. He will have nothing to control until we correct the situation; and it must be corrected. He forgot that each man in a business really wants to and will carry his job if he is given the opportunity.

Of course, there was another error. The management above the merchandising manager had failed through too much delegation and too little control. We all go to national societies' sales-training executive meetings. We spend a lot of time on sales conferences. We spend a lot of money bringing lecturers in. And then we are upset because of the failure of a complete dry run with everyone. Something happens, as happened at that sales conference I attended.

Another factor I would like to mention is incentive, which is very important in delegation and control. There are three kinds of incentive: (1) money, (2) growth in the business, and (3) recognition. Proper incentives at the field sales level can do much to help sales management in accomplishing the necessary controls to produce desired results.

Quite recently we had an experience at Bauer & Black that is of interest because it deals with a particular incentive tool for better sales control, namely, salesmen's compensation.

After an intensive study of many companies, we arrived at a salary and bonus plan that to us represented the strongest available program. Then, with some experience we found that although the plan supplied the needed incentive for most men, there were certain men who were affected entirely too little by the bonus program. We went back to the fundamentals of motivation, which had not been considered carefully enough in our bonus plan. Of the various major motivating factors, *to acquire* (money, economic security) actually ranks low. With many men, the first motivation is *to be recognized* (a place in the sun); and the second, *to excel* (competitive spirit). Our compensation plan did not satisfy sufficiently those two major motivations, and our compensation plan was one of the important factors in getting our job done.

We then developed a very simple arrangement, a club we call the Curity Club. At different times throughout the year, men are assigned tasks which have broad effect on the building of business; and these tasks are assigned values in shares of stock in the Curity

Club. At the end of the year, on the basis of the amount of stock earned by the various men, we select a Curity Club president and board of directors. There is a small monetary reward attached to membership on the Curity Club board, but the primary reward is recognition at the sales conference and the publicity given to the accomplishment of the Curity Club winners each year. We have found that this program, tied to our regular compensation plan, has stepped up over-all sales operating control to a substantial degree. I am certainly not saying we have found *the* answer, but we have definitely found a *better* answer, in this program, than we have had before.

The full potential of the management team will not be released until we find more and better ways to utilize the contributions that can be made by all members of that team; and this requires maximum delegation. That certainly is our objective at Bauer & Black as I am sure it is at most companies today.

In a Metal Fabricating Company

*By Peter P. Wojtul**

If I were asked to set up a salesforce or handle some other problem in sales or marketing, I would first ask a lot of questions of the person who brought the problem to me, to make sure that we both understood our problem and our objectives. I would explore with him the available alternatives, with the advantages and disadvantages of each. If possible, I would ask for actual related experiences. And then, after we had thoroughly discussed all the pertinent facts, I would probably ask him this question, "Well, in view of all this, what do *you* recommend?"

I intend to build my discussion around actual experiences in my

* Mr. Wojtul is Vice President in charge of Sales for the Continental Can Company. Previously, he was general sales manager of the metal division, director of sales research and development, and assistant to the president. He is a member of the board and chairman of the marketing committee of the Can Manufacturers Institute.

own company, the Continental Can Company. The reader may be wondering what those opening sentences have to do with delegation and control in Continental's sales organization. The answer is that those four words, "What do *you* recommend?" following a thorough discussion of all the facts surrounding a problem, are symbolic of the manner in which we expect all sales management in Continental to operate.

Continental has several product divisions; I shall confine myself to the metal or "can division," not only because it is our largest but also because only a few years ago it operated on a highly centralized basis.

Today the reverse is true. We still have some functions that are handled in our home office — not from choice, but because some things must be done in a uniform manner throughout the organization. In our case, pricing is probably the most important of these functions. But even in such matters, the field salesforce is consulted, asked for recommendations, and given every opportunity to participate in the final decisions. In that most important function of selling, getting and holding business or the servicing and handling of accounts, we have decentralized to a high degree.

Only a few years ago, line authority in our company passed down from our officers and department heads in the home office to division department heads and then to department managers in the plants and sales offices. On our organization charts, our district sales managers reported to division general sales managers, who in turn reported to the vice president in charge of sales. That was so on our organization charts.

But, as General Clay indicates in Part I, charts do not always tell the story. In actual practice, the district sales managers reported to various division product sales managers, who handled and were responsible for different product lines. These division sales managers reported to product sales managers in our New York office. In their assigned fields home-office sales managers, who appeared on the charts in staff positions, personally handled many important accounts and exercised a considerable amount of authority over sales managers and salesmen.

Today, the sales organization is set up with district sales managers in full charge of the salesmen and the sales office managers in the territories assigned to them. The district sales managers report to area managers who are in charge of all operations, both sales and manufacturing, in their respective territories. The line of command goes up from the area managers to division vice presidents and then to the executive vice president, all of whom are in charge of both sales and manufacturing operations.

With this type of organization, all sales managers at levels above that of district sales manager — in other words, all the division and home-office sales managers — operate entirely in staff positions. They have no line authority over district sales managers, salesmen, or sales office managers.

This means that we have people in staff positions concerned with different product lines, while the salesmen sell all of them under district managers. It might seem that we would have trouble keeping home-office product managers from stepping on one another's or on the salesmen's toes.

Actually, every product sales manager is fighting for the salesmen's and the district sales managers' time. He is constantly sending them bulletins. He asks why this particular line is not moving or is not moving better, and so on. All of them are really fighting one another for the district sales officer's time. The job of deciding which product is going to get the most attention is the job of the district sales manager.

The product sales manager always has recourse to the general sales manager of the metal division who, in turn, goes up through the line and complains to the executive vice president if he thinks some district sales office is not giving enough attention to a particular product. But basically the product sales manager has got to sell the district men, to get them to do what he wants done with his product.

We do not have any trouble because the district sales manager knows that if the product sales manager has a real complaint, he can get action through the district or the area manager — through the line.

Each of the sales managers at division offices and at the home office is expected to operate in the manner described in the opening paragraph of this section. Whenever a problem comes up from someone in the field, he is expected to bring into the discussion of it all the pertinent facts, data, and previous experience that apply. He participates actively in finding the solution, but he does not make the final decision; that is the responsibility of the line organization. And the best way to ensure that decisions will be made all down the line is to train sales management to make constant use of that question, "What do *you* recommend?" addressed to the field force.

In my opinion, in any organization, or in any department, decentralization is not really practiced until management at the higher levels, whether staff or line, insists on recommendations from the lower levels of the organization before making its own recommendation or decision.

Now, having described briefly our selling organization as it operated a few years ago and as it operates today, I would like to consider a few important aspects of the changes that have taken place.

First, we made two major moves as far as organization charts were concerned. In our first move, in 1948, all sales management positions at the home office were made staff instead of line positions. The organization was advised that all sales managers at the home office no longer exercised any line authority over the division or district sales managers or over the salesmen and, further, that these sales managers had no direct responsibility for obtaining or holding any business.

The second major move was made in the middle of 1952, when area managers were set up, with line responsibility both for district sales offices and for plants. At that time the division sales management positions were made staff positions. The division sales managers were relieved of all line authority over district sales managers and their salesmen.

District sales managers, with their office staffs and salesmen, no longer report to division sales managers, but report directly to area managers. Each area manager reports to a division vice president.

Because of the importance of this position in our setup, I would like to describe it in some detail.

Each area manager has several plants and district sales offices reporting to him. He is fully responsible for all operations of the plants and sales offices assigned to him. The area manager has no sales staff of his own. In each division he is, in effect, a deputy vice president and depends on his division vice president's sales staff for assistance in the operation of his sales district.

The area manager's office is not an office of records and reports. He receives only those reports essential for his knowledge and control of over-all progress and results. The line of communication between district sales offices and division sales managers is not through the area office. In other words, the division sales staffs still work directly with district sales offices on all routine matters. Nevertheless, the area manager is fully responsible for the operating results in his area.

Of course, mere announcement of the change of positions from "line" to "staff" did not accomplish the decentralization and delegation of responsibility that we were seeking. (In fact, while we have done many things to speed up the process of decentralization, it is a never-ending process, and we are still at it.)

In order to implement in fact the changes represented on our organization chart, we prepared a manual outlining the difference between line and staff responsibilities and the relationship between line and staff positions, both in general terms and specifically for each department. Detailed position analyses were drawn up for all positions involved in the reorganization. When these had been published, meetings were held across the country to explain the new relationships and the duties and the responsibilities of the various positions.

In the sales organization, we laid great emphasis on the fact that responsibility for customer accounts, for obtaining and holding sales volume, rested solely with district office personnel. We emphasized also that district sales managers must, in turn, delegate responsibility for accounts to their salesmen. We insisted that every account must be assigned to a salesman capable of handling the account on his own, although, of course, each salesman is expected to use the services of our entire sales and service organization when desirable. But we eliminated "house accounts."

Naturally, we expect home-office and division sales managers still to have considerable contact with customers. We have a large amount of "executive" selling in our business, and many of our customers expect and demand higher-up attention. The responsibility for properly using executives in selling belongs to the district sales office. We expect district sales managers to use and arrange for these higher-level contacts. The district sales manager, however, is never relieved of the primary responsibility even for the accounts that receive a large amount of executive attention.

Moreover, the executives do not take over accounts; rather, they render assistance to the field forces. We try, with success, to avoid weakening the salesman in the eyes of the customer when executive attention is required, by (a) getting the salesman to do the planning, (b) bringing the salesman in wherever possible, and (c) if he is not present, sending him a complete report of the session with the customer so that he knows what is going on.

Very early in our decentralization program — in fact before we made the first change in the organization charts — we set out to strengthen the district sales organization.

To do this, we first set up a strong office force under a capable sales office manager, so that the district sales managers had staff assistance in their own offices and would not be dependent on the division offices for it. We also set up effective selection and training and development programs not only for new men but also for experienced salesmen and district sales managers. We insisted on more frequent and better organized district sales meetings, for training purposes as well as for solving current problems.

We started sending out much more information, particularly background material, to field salesforces through regular weekly letters and frequent bulletins. We try to cover in them everything that will make the field forces better informed about our business, as well as about our customers' businesses.

All this can be summarized by saying that it is our policy that the salesmen should be as well informed about our business as we can possibly make them. We expect them to know not only what is happening but also why certain things are or are not being done.

In addition, in the course of decentralization, all sales control reports were reviewed and overhauled. The revised reports were decided on, not on the basis of what was needed at the division offices or at the home office for control purposes, but on the basis of what the district sales managers and the salesmen needed to do their jobs properly.

The market research and sales analysis departments were reoriented and redirected. They, too, were given as their objective the task of providing district sales offices and salesmen with tools that will help them achieve sales goals.

There are two more elements of the program that I should mention. One is that, in spite of the fact that in our business it is difficult to measure sales performance accurately, we nevertheless have set up a sales incentive system for district sales personnel. (We have so arranged this that it has been very helpful in clearly defining responsibility for servicing national accounts out in the districts.) Second, whenever we had to make a choice, we placed our greatest strength in our line and field positions and filled sales management positions at the head office with the younger, less experienced men. In fact, many staff sales positions at the division offices and at the head office are being used as training positions, in preparation for an assignment to a district sales-manager position.

We went outside the company to fill some home-office sales positions rather than make transfers that would weaken the field salesforce. This, of course, was handled carefully to make sure that it did not have a detrimental effect on the advancement opportunities of the employees we already had. Growth helped considerably; but I should emphasize here that our decentralization and delegation program actually increased considerably the stature of the positions of district sales managers and salesmen without detracting from the importance of the positions of the division and home-office sales managers.

I would not be truthful if I claimed that we did not have to overcome some fear and misgiving on the part of those men whose positions were changed from line to staff. Personal assurances regarding the importance of the staff were naturally received with some skepticism. As time went on, however, the men learned that effectiveness and status do not depend on the line authority that is or is not shown on an organization chart, but depend rather on experience and knowledge of the business and customers. They learned that these would always carry more authority than any line drawn on an organization chart.

Through salary ranges, through the inclusion of many division and home-office sales managers in the company's management incentive plan, and through the inclusion of these men in general company management meetings, we emphasized that the management really meant it when it said that the importance of any person in the company and his contribution to the company's success did not depend on whether the man held a staff or a line position on the organization chart. At the same time we did not for a moment let up on our insistence that the staff managers had to get results through advice, assistance, and counsel, and not through direction of the field force.

So much for the changes that have occurred in our sales organization since we began pushing responsibility, authority, and decision-making down to the field sales organization.

Now the question naturally arises: "Is all this paying off?" With the large growth we have had in the past few years, it is difficult to visualize how we could operate effectively at all if we had not started decentralizing when we did. Results, of course, are what count.

Our sales volume has been growing steadily, and while there is much still to be done, I believe we have a strong, effective sales team. The decentralization program, with all that went to make it up, deserves a major share of the credit for the success that we have had.

The sales effort of any organization, to be most effective, should be tailored to the markets and the customers that it serves. In fact, as far as possible, it should be tailored to fit the personalities of those customers. Obviously, in a large business which serves many customers, the markets and the customers vary widely in nature and change continually. Delegation becomes particularly important in the sales organization, because it provides flexibility and permits the sales team to meet more easily and effectively the changes in markets and in customers.

Actually, I am convinced that the greatest benefit we receive from the policy of delegation is that it gives us this flexibility in two ways.

First, it has made sales effort much more of a team concern. Division and home-office sales managers must operate through district sales offices on customer problems. District offices, in turn, call on division and home-office managers for assistance because they know they will get help and not interference. Secondly, our policy of delegation forces us to put real strength in our field salesforce and to pursue diligently our programs of training, developing, and informing our sales organization at all levels, but particularly in the district sales offices.

I know of no better way to train salesmen and district sales managers than to insist that division and home-office sales managers and also line executives make frequent use of that four-word question: "What do *you* recommend?"

In a Steel Company

*By R. W. Helms**

You may very well expect that as a sales representative of a steel company I would discuss this problem as it would apply to basic steel. I doubt if in our steel sales there is anything unique in our

* Mr. Helms is Assistant General Manager of Sales for the Republic Steel Corporation. He was branch manager of the Berger Manufacturing Company of Dallas, Texas, until 1929; assistant sales manager and general sales manager of the Berger Division of Republic Steel from 1934 to 1953; and assumed his present position in July 1953.

supervisory or control methods. Instead of discussing our basic steel methods, I shall take up in detail a single, specialized phase of our business.

The Republic Steel Corporation sells its basic steel products through normal channels — to be specific, through its own district sales offices and salesmen. Republic manufactures a wide variety of steel products — bars, sheets, strip, and so forth; and it has seven separate manufacturing divisions, the majority of which have their own, independent sales organizations.

The Berger Manufacturing Division, with which I was associated for a great number of years, has five departmental sales divisions, one of which I shall consider here. Berger Division is a fabricator from flat rolled products, producing steel lockers, steel shelving, office furniture and equipment, special contract items (including voting machines and baby incubators), and Republic Steel Kitchens. It is the sales organization for the last named product that I will discuss here. It is an interesting product to us, not only because it represents a large tonnage consumption, but also because it is one of the few products we sell which can be identified in a home.

We had manufactured steel kitchen cabinets for several years and had distributed them through plumbing supply jobbers. Frankly, we were doing more of an industrial merchandising job with them. A look at our kitchen cabinet sales volume for 1945 and 1946 showed that we were not doing a satisfactory volume. We wanted to reach a bigger percentage of the market and therefore found it necessary to revise our sales methods.

We called in a corps of experts and started out to find what the housewife wants in the way of kitchen cabinets, the best way to sell them, the services involved, and so forth.

We employed a company to design a line which would meet housewives' needs; we set up a tooling program to make the product. We decided that since Republic was a well-known name, we would call the cabinets Republic Steel Kitchens.

Our next step was to set up a sales organization to appoint, train, and serve distributor and dealer outlets. Since we had no merchandising salesmen in our organization, we had to employ men with appliance sales and merchandising experience. What were these men supposed to do?

We undertook job descriptions for this new sales personnel, for the distributor, and for the dealer. This was done carefully because our sales control and direction were to be built around these job descriptions. It is my considered opinion that in too many cases salesmen do not know what they are doing, why they are doing it, and for whom they are doing it. We wrote down specifically the things (32 in number) that this specialty salesman was to do. He then knew what his job was when he came to work for us. These were his functions and his responsibilities.

One job description outlined in detail all the responsibilities of the district manager. It was a measuring stick by which we would control his activity and determine his effectiveness. Sales volume was to be an important measure of a man's effectiveness, but we believed there were other measures too, which should not be ignored. The description was set up as follows:

1 — Basic Objective. To assist the distributors within his territory by enthusiastic leadership to attain a high level of sales of Republic Steel Kitchens. Sales and expense quotas assigned on basis of percentage of total market in each territory.

2 — Duties and Responsibilities. Responsible for the selection, development, training, and leadership of distributor outlets to assure a high level of sales and co-ordination of distributor — Republic Steel Kitchen policies as established by Distributor Franchise Agreement.

3 — Co-operate with distributors in the classroom training of all distributor Retail Supervisors.

4 — Co-operate with the distributors in conducting on-the-job training of the Retail Supervisors.

5 — Make regularly scheduled calls on each distributor.

6 — Set up, with the distributors, special dealer contacts to be made with the distributors' Retail Supervisors.

7 — Set up, with the co-operation of the distributors, sales meetings covering new advertising, promotion, product, et cetera campaigns or other important matters.

8 — Make quarterly evaluation report of the territory and the sales activities of the distributors.
9 — Quarterly evaluation of territory and the distributors' dealer sales activities.
10 — Co-operate with the distributors in the checking of the Retail Supervisors' dealers' monthly forecasts.
11 — Prepare monthly forecast for transmission to his Sales Manager.
12 — Assist the distributors in the construction of monthly co-op advertising reports.
13 — Co-operate with the distributors in the analysis and counseling of Retail Supervisors regarding daily call reports.
14 — Co-operate with the distributors in the compiling and maintenance of a complete list of all potential dealers the distributors might sell.
15 — Co-operate with the distributors in the compiling of information of market activities which might affect the distributors' competitive position.
16 — Co-operate with the distributors' Retail Supervisors in the selection of new dealers.
17 — Co-operate with the distributors in the operation of the company-planned dealer sales training program as provided for in the Distributor and Dealer Franchise Agreement.
18 — Recommend and co-operate with the distributors in the initiating of sales-stimulating contests.
19 — Cultivate all the people in each distributor's business and induce them to become a part of the team.
20 — Assist the distributors in their consumer selling activities.
21 — Assist the distributors in the compiling of a mailing list.
22 — Activities with contractors falling within the Territorial Jurisdiction of the distributors.
23 — Activities with other personnel within each distributor's business.
24 — Assist the distributors' Advertising and Sales Promotion Departments.
25 — Assist the distributors' Warehouse Managers.
26 — Responsible for the implementation and supervision of company policy as it applies to the functions to be carried on at the District Supervisor's level.
27 — Responsible for normal marketing activities in nonselling fields, such as market studies and market research, product development, distribution, competition, sales records, et cetera.
28 — Reporting activities — all reports to be sent to Sales Manager.
29 — Prepare complaint reports and make recommendations for adjustments.

30 — Prepare reports covering special test and report on the outcome.
31 — Attend regularly scheduled sales meetings.
32 — Responsible for his own personal development in the field of community leadership, moral ethics, business leadership, human relationships and the development of a sympathetic and yet objective attitude toward those with whom he comes in normal contact.

The same procedure was used for job evaluation for the distributors and the dealers. The district manager is required to check the performance of the distributor against the appropriate job description; the distributor checks the dealer's performance against his job description.

The ink was hardly dry before we had made some changes in the job description — duties were either taken from or added to. We then had a measuring stick for all men in this classification. A fair and reasonably accurate measuring of sales performance is the one big problem of sales management.

How do you find out whether a man is a good salesman? Is he good when his dollar volume is high and his sales expense low? Or is there more to a salesman's job, a district manager's job, a vice president's job when it comes to the sales field? We feel that there is, and that is why we set up this job description as the measuring stick of his success.

I know from almost 30 years' experience in working with district and sales offices that you are licked if you have nothing to talk about except generalities. You go in to see your sales offices and if you only talk generalities, all you ever hear is something about weather; and, if you do succeed in channeling the conversation to business, all you get is a standard reply — "the competition is terrific, and our prices are too high." If you try to answer "generalities" you will convince no one — not even yourself.

You have to have something specific to say, if it's only "How far is it from Syracuse to Rochester?" Even that is better than generalities such as "Let's all get our shoulders behind the wheel and bring in some sales." This list of specific things a salesman should be doing that we have developed not only helps us to spot his strengths and weaknesses but to talk to him specifically about how he can improve his performance.

It is my considered opinion that too much sales direction and control has centered around the sales quota (and perhaps the traveling expenses) of most salesmen; a dollar sales quota is set up for the salesman and then, if he makes his goal, too often it is assumed that the job is well done. Present-day selling does not permit looking only at the day's dollar volume. In appliance merchandising—and this also applies to industrial selling—continued relationship between buyer and seller is a very important factor. Future sales planning is the responsibility of each salesman; there are a great many things over and above the day-to-day dollar order that a salesman must do if he is to be successful.

The problem of most sales managers is to find a set of standards by which salesmen can be gauged. This can be done effectively by setting up standards or—as I have called it—a job description for each man with selling responsibility.

I certainly would not recommend this as the only method of sales control, sales regulation, or sales communication. But I do say that as an adjunct in sales control, regulation, and communication it is quite helpful.

Most people—and that includes all of us—are likely to be surprised when we see what our own specific duties are, what we are supposed to do in our day-to-day work. Not that knowing what we are supposed to do means that we will always get it done. I am sure others have the same trouble I do. I come to work with a schedule all planned, then three men come in and the program is changed. Nothing happened that I planned on. But, just the same, I need those measuring sticks for myself and for my people. I have something specific to work with, and it does help me to get proper performance.

A well-disciplined salesman is a good salesman—one who has a great variety of responsibilities which can be checked regularly. He is easily directed, and his discipline makes the job of sales manager interesting, stimulating, and satisfying.

In an Oil Company

*By Harry J. Kennedy**

The seven chapters in the second part of this book are intended to move the treatment of the theme of delegation and control from the general to the specific. To be consistent with such a purpose, I shall confine myself to a narrow area of the subject and discuss just one thought. That thought is this: in all our preoccupation with effective delegation and control, and by our silence on personal contact as a "control tool" in selling, we seem to be laying away, *as outmoded,* that one control that energizes all the rest. Many writers in such books as this do not even honor it by mention. Many managers tend to overlook it for newer and shinier (and therefore presumably sharper) control tools.

Let us look first at this proposition in general terms; subsequently I shall try to illustrate it by reference to my own company.

The idea of delegation and control is really not new in the field of organization. We have simply begun to talk about it more in business since bigness began to complicate life. But to the sales supervisor (at any level) who long since has had his fill of airports and railroad stations at all hours of the day and night, there is something of a new dawn in the imperfectly understood notion that effective delegation, control reports, predigested statistical studies, and a dictating machine constitute the modern, scientific trappings of a sales executive. We owe it to these men to carry the thinking on decentralization through and to tell the whole story.

Personal contact for problem solving, with its synthesis of partly formed ideas into inventiveness, can too easily be regarded as not

* Mr. Kennedy is Vice President of the Continental Oil Company, in charge of marketing. He started his career in the Marland Oil Company, which later changed its name to Continental, and in 1930 he was made general sales manager of Continental, taking the position he now holds in April 1936. In addition, Mr. Kennedy is a member of the general committee of marketing and a past marketing vice president and president of the American Petroleum Institute.

a control tool because it is not something that is made up from the cards that come out of a punched-card machine.

Is this exaggeration? Let the reader stop and think of what he reads and hears. At general industrial seminars and big marketing conferences, at conventions in particular industries, the interest seems to center more and more on the forms and procedures for control reports to spot the problem areas, and less and less on generating the inventive ingenuity to lick the problems. I do not scorn control reports or anything else which brings the sales supervisor facts. They are, however, only indicators of direction or speed which the supervisor may use as guides in the creation of ideas for plans of action.

The professional practitioners in the field of organization theory are the leading offenders (although certainly innocent ones) in what I see as a misplacing of emphasis. They have invented a jargon that beguiles amateurs into thinking that delegation and control are more technical than they are. Actually, these concepts are rather simple if we use some of the old words instead of the new ones.

Let us take a quick look at two of the sayings about delegation and control currently in vogue:

1. Effective delegation is not abdication.
2. The establishment of exactly countervailing controls is implicit in effective delegation.

I agree with both statements, and stripped of semantics they both mean about the same thing; but I could not have agreed without translating them to see what they mean. What do such things really say to an old-fashioned sales executive like me, and to the sales supervisors who are on my team?

In plain words, they say that we cannot chuck *our* responsibilities by placing them on our subordinates. Neither do we divest ourselves of our authority by sharing it with our men. This remains true no matter to what degree we divide up our assignment. Here is a new version of the old story of the loaves and fishes. No matter how much authority or responsibility we give out, we still have the same amount left.

But what are the consequences of our having to remain fully responsible in spite of all our delegating? Let us examine this to see what we can discover that would have meaning for *any* sales supervisor. To be faithful to our repsonsibilities, we cannot turn away and ignore what occurs after we delegate. We must observe. We must inspect. We must encourage. We must supervise. In short, we must *control;* and since our authority also still remains, we can and will do so.

Why should we not speak out and demonstrate this train of thought to our travel-weary sales supervisor? He can see how it fits him. He has no uncertainty about the meaning of supervision. If control means supervision and if supervision means control, the man trained in marketing does not need to be told that they both mean personal contact. The trouble is that in our playing with the fancy modern terms we seem to have lost sight of some of the relationship between control and supervision. Let us recapture it by reducing some of our erudition to plain old-fashioned phrases and including in them some respectful words about personal contact as the "guts" of it all.

Continual, frequent personal contact between all marketing supervisors and subordinates, right through all levels of rank, makes two great contributions in the area of effective delegation and control, one or both of which are sometimes forgotten:

(1) Personal contact facilitates and encourages the tactful administration of controls when they are concerned with correction and improvement. Many superiors do not seem to realize that true tactfulness and consideration are vital to constructive relationships on such matters. To help toward this realization, some professional ought to launch a twin of that saying I just quoted, namely, "Effective delegation is not abdication." Its counterpart might well be: *"Effective control is not usurpation."*

To commit unjust encroachments in disregard of delegations is certainly usurpation and the epitome of tactlessness as well. Controls administered without sensitivity to a subordinate's feelings are bitterly destructive. When supervision becomes interference, leadership is lost. When the Boss (and the word fits in this context) figuratively or literally stands over his man's shoulder and controls too aggressively or too closely, there is usurpation. Formal administration of controls by mail, or even by telephone, always runs the risk of being construed as usurpation. A too formal person-to-person relationship is likely to be misunderstood too.

In creating a good atmosphere for correction and improvement nothing susbtitutes for the intimacy and informality that grow out of frequent personal contact. With the right personal contact well established, and with mutual good will flourishing, the skilled supervisor can induce all the suggestions to come his way instead of letting them go the other way carrying the sting of criticism. The habit of taking the initiative then is formed in the subordinate, and valuable, candid criticism of plans that are not working well can be secured from him, unstifled by awe or fear of the Boss.

(2) The second of the two great contributions made by continual, frequent personal contact has already been alluded to. It is the creation of favorable conditions for the synthesis of ideas on solving problems. It is the catalyst that facilitates the transformation of two or three separately worthless thoughts into a creative idea.

General Electric recently ran an advertisement headlined, "Can Inventiveness Be Increased?" Concerning the student in a special group which was being trained for improved inventiveness, these sentences appeared:

> "He also learns that working with other creative people can be highly stimulating, and that it often pays to bring a number of minds to bear on a project. One man's hunch inspires another; the half-formed idea of a third is made whole by a fourth; the amusing 'notion' tossed out almost as a joke leads to a solution . . . The men who have attended the course continue to develop new processes and patentable ideas at an average rate almost three times that of nongraduates."

I do not believe I need to labor any further this contribution to a creative potential which is supplied by personal contact.

Now let me illustrate in terms of the specific situation of Continental Oil. What actually goes on during these personal contacts, and what does the *company* get from them?

Through each contact we are seeking principally to discover the degree of the salesman's success in achieving the objective set up for him or for his territory. From conferring with the men we have worked out those objectives. They are *not* quotas that the sales manager in the home office sends down the line, which the men generally do not like.

The controlling in the personal contacts consists of a very casual and informal discussion between the man in charge and two or three levels of supervision. The subordinates are led to show their degree of success in the attainment of objectives. If they are not reaching them, embarrassing questions really do not need to be asked. The man wants to explain why he is not reaching them. If the relationship is right, he will not only explain his failure to meet his objectives, but he will also point out some of the things that are wrong with the details of the objectives as they are set up. He will suggest some changes.

Out of the discussion with him a decision is reached concerning what may be done to improve the arrangement. That decision may be made in an automobile; it may be made over dinner.

There is a comment Professor Edmund P. Learned made in one of his classes which I attended. We had a tough problem to wrestle with, and Professor Learned knew there was a party that evening. I remember he said that he believed strongly that maturation of thought can take place even in the most highly social of situations. So, across the table where there is light informality and personal intimacy, the thought process may reach its zenith.

We try to find out what a man thinks is wrong. We try to get his ideas — Mr. Wojtul has used the expression, "What do *you* recommend?" We seek to lead rather than drive.

By this method, we have controls stimulated largely by the men who are being controlled. They participate in the formulation of plans and objectives, and they like the plans and objectives because they have had a part in formulating them. They are stimulated rather than depressed by the controls.

In other words, what we are trying to control through personal contact is a man's achievement of his objectives. We may have to get into a discussion of his expenses, for instance; but if they are above his budget, he knows that before he sees us. We try to let him have a chance to bring the subject up rather than jump on him. It is out of these discussions that we control the salesman's handling of his job.

Keeping the man on the firing line in contact with those above can pay off materially. Here is an illustration showing the value of the initiative and originality of the one man who knows more about his problems than anybody sitting up in a tower — the salesman. He lives with them. He fights to meet his objectives, and he meets difficulties. He has ideas about how to meet them, and they don't always work. But sometimes they do:

Back in prohibition days, we had a motor oil which was made with the use of an additive, one of the first in the industry. The additive gave the oil not only increased oiliness but also the property of penetrating into metal surfaces. We had very definite proof of it from the University of Illinois physics laboratory. The laboratory made X-ray photographs which we used to prove that this oil used in an engine provided a permanent adsorbed film.

Our advertising agency, in the tower, wrote copy about the oil having penetrating lubricity. That meant nothing to most of the men on the firing line, particularly to the man on the service station driveway trying to sell the oil to motorists. The program did not work.

However, we discovered from "control reports" that one district was way over its objective. Why? A supervisor went to find out. He discovered that there was one service station operator who had begun to talk about that penetrative lubricity in different terms. He pointed out that if a man ran his motor with five quarts of this oil for a few hundred miles, then he couldn't drain the five quarts out. He could only drain four; and if he put four more in, the gauge stick read "full." It was a rough but clear demonstration that about one quart of this oil actually clung to the inside of the lubricated surfaces of the engine, and this was a fact previously established by our research engineers.

This man, instead of talking about penetrative lubricity, said that there was a quart of oil that remained in the engine; it was hidden. Then he started talking about the "hidden quart." And in prohibition days "hidden quart" was a meaningful phrase. That man was selling our new oil, while others could not.

The district manager had presented the idea to the other service stations in the district, and the whole district was benefiting from it. When the home office found out what was happening, we handed the idea to our advertising agents. They prepared a whole campaign on it which ran for several years. All this was more than 20 years ago, but whenever we have made surveys of consumer understanding since (and as late as just this year), some consumers still "play back" to us the "hidden quart" phrase. The best ideas usually come from the man way down the line if control techniques have encouraged him to create and suggest.

I will close by quoting a brief line, which I think adds support to what may, by now, have become tiresome with my repetition — the fact that continual, frequent personal contact serves as a vital tool in effective control. The line is one credited to Secretary of the Treasury George Humphrey, "The best fertilizer is the footprints of the boss."

Questions about Delegation

*An Open Discussion**

From the floor: Delegation is a fine idea. But how far can you go? I should like to ask some specific questions about pricing. Does your staff or your line set price policy? Is the execution of price competition delegated? If so, how far? How do you control price strategy when control of operations is decentralized? How can you delegate authority to lower-level executives for departure from prices to meet special considerations? Can you maintain control over profit margins? If profits can be used as a measure of delegation, as Mr. Yntema said, (Part I), why cannot pricing be delegated more fully and the over-all results — sales volume and profits — be included in judging a sales manager's capabilities?

Or, to put it all in one question: *To what extent do you delegate price strategy or price decisions or price exceptions?*

Mr. Kennedy: In our company we do a great deal of delegating of authority and responsibility on prices. This is something of an

* Businessmen present at the panel session on which this chapter is based raised certain questions which brought about the interplay of ideas reported more or less verbatim in this section.

innovation in our industry, where prices have been strictly controlled by tradition for many, many years, particularly in the big companies covering large geographical areas, whose competitive impact is widespread and frequently forceful.

We decentralized our management six years ago. We changed it from strictly a line organization with very little staff into a regional setup in which each regional general manager runs a small Continental Oil Company in an area of four or five states. He is responsible for the profits of that region. To those men we have delegated authority on prices having to do with our tank-wagon structure — the prices at which we sell to dealers and to farmers.

The regional offices have, in turn, delegated some of that authority to the division offices, the next unit in the regional breakdown.

For defensive action against a competitor's lower price, there is practically no restriction on the division manager. On a general increase in price the general economics involved have to be considered more than on a defense against a lower price. Also, in our business, prices, particularly when they go up, are political issues. For these reasons, a general increase cannot be approved in the regional offices. It must come to the headquarters office for consideration, and the general sales manager or else one of his two assistants must pass on it.

In bulk sales, where we may sell several carloads or barge loads of gasoline, or in heating oil, the price limitation is stricter because there we are dealing with much more sensitive price markets. Prices can be changed only by the general sales manager. In most large companies, pricing control on everything is still held in the main office, and in some instances I suspect that the board of directors has to pass on any change. We have gone farther in delegating pricing.

Mr. Helms: Frankly, my heart bleeds for the man who submitted that question. He must have been a district or branch manager, and I know just exactly how he feels when his hands are tied. Specifically, in our company the control of prices up or down is entirely in the main office. No jurisdiction is given to people in the field for moving in or out of a price situation. In other words, any change has to be cleared at the head office before action can be taken on it.

MR. WOJTUL: Pricing in our company is delegated down to the product division, but no further. Each product division determines its prices. Pricing for the metals division is done in the home office. We have uniform prices on cans everywhere east of the Rockies and another uniform schedule west of the Rockies. We have often given this problem consideration, and we have thought about trying to give some authority down the line, but we do not know just how to do it. With the same prices used in a whole area, with many national accounts, and with plants all over the country, I do not think there *is* any way to do it. I do not see how pricing authority can be delegated in our business beyond the product divisions.

MR. BROWN: As for what Mr. Helms said, his heart bleeds for the district managers; my heart bleeds for me. We have to bring in a Philadelphia lawyer in our business to tell us what we can do and what we cannot do with our prices. After we arrive at the pricing, authority to vary it is not delegated.

MR. HANSEN: I would like to add one sentence to this discussion. Mr. Yntema's method of decentralizing to profit centers is a very useful one in many cases; but when we use it, we have to realize that profit-success isn't really the final measure of success because control over price tends to be centralized, and price obviously affects profits.

FROM THE FLOOR: Another aspect of delegation bothers me — the matter of personnel. How can you detect and develop sales administrators in contrast to just good salesmen? How do you go about building your personnel in a decentralized organization? How do you know that a man in one of the decentralized units has sufficient training and/or ability to be promoted into other separate decentralized units? Sometimes we run into this kind of problem when we have a salesman who is very successful in, say, the central division. There may be no opportunities for promotion there. He might be used in the western division, but under decentralized operation should you interfere with the central division and take him out, or is he entirely under the control of the divisional executive?

Or, to put the problem together in one sentence: ***Where you decentralize responsibilities, how do you keep track of the people in the decentralized operations?***

Mr. Kennedy: It is a very difficult thing in a decentralized organization to keep track of the men in the lower ranks beyond the regional officer's own watching of those men. However, when a man moves up to the position in our company of district manager or assistant division manager, he may have charge of our activity in one state, perhaps a half or a third of a division. That man, by reason of our practice of continual and frequent contact, becomes pretty well known to those of us who have an interest in his promotion to a higher position, possibly in another region.

We have proceeded with considerable confidence, but it is admittedly difficult to ensure that a young man in his first three to five years with the company gets a fair shake and a promotion, which may not be available in his own division, but which does open up in another division halfway across the country from him.

Mr. Wojtul: I think we are quite fortunate in our setup. We have a sales development plan, and as part of the plan a list is constantly maintained of the men in our district sales offices who are considered potential sales managers. The list is made up by our sales manager who sits down and discusses these men with their superiors to determine whether they should or should not be put on the list.

We also use merit-rating forms to appraise the men. Those are not the final answer. We have very close contact with all our sales managers, and all of them are on a first-name basis with all except our newest salesmen. So we think we know the men who are available and eligible for promotion.

Mr. Brown: I think this is a very good question because we ran right into the problem when we decentralized. We have in the neighborhood of 300 salesmen, and, as I mentioned earlier, our philosophy is one of building our own organization. We hire young men and bring them up in the business. When we went into the program of decentralization, we found that there was a tendency to "hang on." So we placed one man in charge of our development program to co-ordinate all the material on manpower. This man has no line responsibility, but he frequently goes to the various managers saying, "Here are some available assignments. Who are your best candidates?" The strength of our business is obviously giving growth to these good, young men; and we have broken away from that tendency to hold the man for the job. We now hold the man and make the transfer.

FROM THE FLOOR: I am still bothered about just what sales decisions can be delegated. *What do you delegate—pricing, product policy, inventories, advertising, selection of salesmen?*

MR. KENNEDY: In our business we delegate a great deal of authority in the phase of our marketing which we call "sales operations." We have a considerable physical expansion program involving capital invested in construction of service stations, purchase of service station sites, and general expansion in both old and new communities. Authority to spend money on those projects is very widely delegated *within certain limits as to the number of years to pay out.* If the formula for payout meets the requirements, the field people have a great deal of authority for spending money on these projects. Of course, it is budgeted in advance, and they cannot spend more than is in the budget, but the decision as to where to spend it is liberally delegated.

As I have already mentioned, the limitations as far as pricing is concerned are much fewer than they were a few years ago. We attempt to delegate nearly everything else, to the regional offices particularly.

MR. HELMS: At Republic a department sales head must set up his advertising budget, for example, and have it approved. He can vary that budget only if the variation does not affect the total. He might have $100,000 that he was going to spend in equal parts for literature and advertising. During the year, because of some good and sufficient reason, he might want to put more into advertising and less into literature, and he can do that without asking anybody for approval.

As for sales control, pay raises, merit wages, and so forth, those are all referred to the general office, not the district office. Again, basically, in our operation most of the direct control is in the head office.

MR. WOJTUL: I don't know if I can quickly list here all the areas in which we delegate, but one of our primary principles is to make the district sales offices fully responsible. They determine the plan to be used in going after any piece of business. They determine who is going to call on that account, what kind of service we are going to give or offer, what gimmicks we are going to use, the advantages we are going to show to get a particular piece of business.

The district managers also determine what they want produced. They give the estimates to the plant for what the plant is to put into stock. They determine the type and amount of service customers get. They settle all claims except those that run into very big amounts. They determine which men in their districts will attend courses every so often. Training responsibility is delegated to them.

MR. BROWN: We delegate hiring and selection for advancement to a high degree. We also delegate the establishment of distributors, and that is an important part of our business. The man who has to produce the volume and who is responsible for the area decides who should be his distributors.

MR. HANSEN: I should like to add one remark here. I heard a very interesting discussion this spring by the advertising manager for one of the large manufacturers of rubber tires. He said that his company had decentralized advertising decisions to the extent that while the home office did all the planning and scheduling in the development of national media, magazines, network radio and television, the advertising in all local media was under the control of the regional managers. They made all the decisions on whether or not they wanted radio or newspapers, when and where. What they controlled, of course, had to be kept within the total appropriation for the period.

Conclusion

*By Harry L. Hansen**

There are certain themes running through all the experience represented in this chapter, and I think these themes are fundamental to the concept and act of decentralization. Before pointing them up, I will record an anecdote which illustrates, if in a negative way, the initiative a salesman may take if he is left free to do so:

The Harvard Business School once had a case involving Standard Brands' selling of photographic film to grocery stores from its trucks. We had a good deal of useful discussion on the case in classes, and we used it once as an examination. Later we went back to the Boston district office to see how the company was doing.

The manager said, "Sit down and I'll tell you an interesting story. I was looking over my control reports recently and I noticed that we weren't selling very much film in one of our districts, and everywhere else it was going fine. The next time I went to this branch, I met the salesman and said, 'I'd like to ride around on the truck with you.'

"As I was riding with the driver, a personable young fellow, I asked him, 'How are you doing on your film sales?'

"He said, 'Not very well. You know, that won't work.'

" 'How do you know that?' I asked.

" 'Well, as you know, this is just a summer job for me. I'm a student at the Harvard Business School. We've analyzed this case down there and come to the conclusion that there's no future in this film business.'!"

In general, however, I think it is safe to say that if salesmen are left to exercise their own judgment, always subject to reasonable controls, the company will benefit in many ways in the long run.

The growth of our economy and the increasing scale of the firm's operations are forcing decentralization of decision-making and review of existing control methods. While there may be some "faddism" in the current interest in delegation and control, there is, unmistakably, an underlying trend to decentralization.

* Mr. Hansen, who served as moderator of the panel session on which this chapter is based, is Professor of Business Administration, Harvard Business School.

Briefly, the following would appear to be the important factors in a successful decentralization program:

1. The proper selection and training of men to operate under the program. It is a commonplace observation that too often management techniques are stuck onto organizations like adhesive tape. People make techniques perform; techniques do not make people perform.

2. The establishment of job descriptions which define as carefully as possible the limits of authority and responsibility at different organizational levels. While such descriptions will naturally be drawn up when a decentralization program is originated, it is necessary to see that these limits are continually refined and improved with experience. Effective, decentralized decision-making and useful control measures must be nurtured. They obviously cannot be created by decree, nor do they result from short-run indoctrination programs.

3. The realization that decentralization means increased attention to the passing down of information to the field organization. Furthermore, decentralization of decision-making requires decentralization of decision-assisting staff services.

4. A successful blend of personal dealing and impersonal report control. It is a mistake to regard these two forms of control as interchangeable. They are not; they are complementary. Reports can never replace the understanding which results from face-to-face dealing; face-to-face dealing can never achieve the impartiality nor compel the study of facts as the statistical report does. In fact, impersonal reports give the point to personal control.

5. The creation of the attitude that decentralized decision-making is really wanted by top management. This involves willingness to bear the cost of mistakes if these are necessary to demonstrate the sincerity of the objective.

There are three questions about the application of the decentralization concept which the authors of the preceding sections have suggested:

(1) How does one tell people what is expected of them in such a way that they understand?

The answer to this question was given to us long ago in the

Bible—"By their fruits ye shall know them." Works, not words, are important. Mr. Wojtul has suggested the question: "What do *you* recommend?" In the context of this summary I would rephrase that slightly to "What is your *decision?*" This is different from a question like "What are the facts?" The former requires lower executive levels to commit themselves; the latter implies that the higher level will make the decision.

Few things are more demoralizing to an organization than a management which tells subordinates that they have the responsibility and authority for decisions and then pre-empts this right for reasons which are, or appear to be, arbitrary. Perhaps the most positive proof management can give that delegation is sincere is to stand by and not interfere while a man makes a bad decision.

(2) How does one develop the ability to discriminate between decisions which can be made locally and those which must be referred to higher authority?

This is a function of experience and formal training. There is no need to comment on experience; by it I mean the results of being involved in many decisions and of being coached by subordinates as well as superiors. We sometimes forget that education can come up the ladder as well as go down. As for formal training, may I remind many readers that they are products of a kind of education called the case method, that business schools have no patent on that method, and that they can themselves apply that kind of training within their own organizations.

(3) How does one create willingness to assume the risks of decentralized decision-making?

Association of the decision-makers and advisers must be as friendly and informal as possible in order to nurture a feeling of *mutual understanding and confidence*. Otherwise uncertainty as to the reactions of higher echelons will lead to either (a) unwillingness to make decisions and greater reliance on headquarters staff sections in order to compromise headquarters into sharing responsibility for the decision; or (b) emotional defense of decisions which have been proved wrong—with all the disruptive consequences of such a defense.

EFFECTIVE DELEGATION AND CONTROL IN SMALLER BUSINESSES

Introduction

*By Paul Donham**

This chapter deals with the need for and extent of effective delegation and control in smaller businesses, particularly in growth situations. When this subject is considered, the first question that comes to mind is: "What is meant by 'smaller businesses'?" In order to avoid confusion we have chosen rather arbitrarily the definition established by the Committee for Economic Development, a definition which is qualitative rather than quantitative, which provides elastic criteria, and which thus seems highly suitable for this chapter's purposes.

The CED says that "usually a small business will show two or more of the following:

"(1) Management is independent; usually the managers are also owners.
"(2) Capital is supplied and ownership held by an individual or small group.
"(3) Area of operations is mainly local; markets need not be local.
"(4) The business is small when compared to the biggest units in its field."

Many readers will ask: "Why delegate?" Others may question: "How far?" Some will be troubled by the problem of determining at what point in a company's growth delegation and control be-

* Mr. Donham, who served as moderator of the panel session on which this chapter is based, is Lecturer in Business Administration, Harvard Business School. Previously he served in various capacities with American Steel and Wire Company and with Owens-Corning Fiberglas Corporation, and has been for a number of years a consultant to small business.

come important. How formalized need they be? What are the risks, and how are they minimized?

The statement is often made that the No. 1 problem of small business is management. Presumably this refers to the quality of management, and the question arises whether delegation and control can be used successfully as training devices to upgrade the quality of the management team.

Others have said that time is the No. 1 problem of small business. Professor Hoad of Michigan refers to the "problems arising out of small business management's difficulty in finding time to manage."[1] Again, the question arises: To what extent may delegation and control serve to relieve the pressing demands on the time of the small-business executive, permitting him to become more effective in, for example, long-range planning?

In many instances small businesses are started and operated by men experienced in only one function. Can they, using the techniques of delegation and control, build a management team which will compensate for their deficiencies and limitations?

Finally we may ask if in small businesses the problem is not one of sharing rather than one of delegating and controlling. We might also consider the importance of that intangible factor, "leadership." If the full potential of the management team in a small business is to be realized, does leadership perhaps far outweigh in importance any policies and procedures, formal or informal, for delegation and control?

Such are the questions to be discussed in this chapter.

[1] *Proceedings of the Ten Weekly Seminars on the Problems of Small Business;* College of Business Administration, Atlanta Division, University of Georgia; October 2–December 4, 1951; p. 57.

Basic Principles

*By Robert E. Worden**

It is difficult, of course, to discuss in a brief space so broad a subject as this one, applying as it does to two of the most perplexing problems of the day in management and economic philosophy:

(1) How is it possible to delegate effectively in a small business, where the number of competent subordinate personnel is limited and they are seldom functionally specialized?

(2) In what ways can an enterprise of limited personnel develop, engineer, and maintain the detailed controls required to pinpoint general and/or specific areas requiring immediate and dynamic managerial attention?

There are, however, certain *basic principles* that apply, and I should like to point primarily to these — and to the particular strengths and weaknesses of small business in delegating responsibilities and authority, and in maintaining adequate administrative and operating controls.

First, let us define the management process, which, in both philosophy and scientific principle, is the same for any company regardless of size or type. To put it simply, management, wherever two or more people work together, is the process of getting things done successfully, at a profit, through the co-ordinated effort of subordinate personnel. Specifically, the management process begins with planning and ends with control. Somewhere in between, the ranking executive delegates to others, who execute his instructions or their responsibilities as defined. Therefore, no discussion dealing with problems of control will be adequate unless we look first to the responsibilities for planning and establishing the objectives, schedules, and standards by which actual achievement is measured and hence controlled.

* Mr. Worden is a Partner in Worden & Risberg, a firm of consulting management engineers and industrial managers, in Philadelphia, which he formed in 1945. Previously he was associated with Campbell Soup Company.

We are concerned here particularly with discussion of effective delegation and control in smaller businesses. There cannot be adequate delegation or control, even in a small business, until the objectives of the enterprise are properly defined and the organization structure properly set up — to assure that the business will receive the necessary attention to planning for market exploitation, product improvement, new product development, capital expenditures, production scheduling, and so on.

In each of the approximately 50 small businesses my firm has dealt with in the last several years, the Achilles' heel has been failure to organize and plan adequately. We may write about delegating and controlling, but we are acting foolishly if we try to do either without an adequate organizational and planning job first. Even small companies cannot afford to grow like Topsy.

Many years ago as they watched General Motors Corporation growing, people wondered how any one company could get so large. Some day, the soothsayers pointed out, General Motors would grow too big! You all know the result — through sound organizational methods, through unimpeachable planning, General Motors has grown to be one of the world's greatest commercial institutions. Today, these same soothsayers are predicting that little businesses cannot survive — that big corporations are squeezing them out. One day we are afraid of bigness; the next we are sensitive to smallness; in both cases the thinking is faulty, based as it is primarily on inadequate understanding of the principles at play.

This is not the time to define the many areas where small businesses are better equipped to do a job than bigger ones. Suffice it to say that there are places and situations where a small company has tremendous advantages over a larger institution, and more situations where a smaller company has few, if any, handicaps in the face of large-corporation competition.

Strangely enough, many of the people who are most pessimistic about the future of small business are entrepreneurs and operators of small companies, in many instances poorly trained and uninformed, who enjoy passing the buck to "situations beyond their control." Needless to say — or to emphasize — the strength of a small company depends largely on the caliber of its top leadership — on the intellectual capacity of this leadership and on its courage to face difficult competitive situations with calm resolve.

When I speak of defining objectives and organization structure for a small company, I am sure I scare most small businessmen. But if one of these men runs the home-town laundry, then he must decide what market he is going to serve, what kind of laundry work he is going to do, how he intends to grow, what new services he intends to add and when, and so on. This is the kind of planning he must do, and this is the kind of planning that small businessmen often fail to do.

As to organization structure, maybe the boss will run the laundry equipment with a helper; perhaps part of the time he will drive the truck; perhaps, for one reason or another, he has decided to incorporate and has to be president, vice president, and secretary-treasurer. In other words, he wears more than one hat. Let him wear as many hats as he wants; he should still lay out *on paper* an organization structure as comprehensive, in principle, as that of the biggest business in the field; and every time he wears a particular hat, he should try to do the job of president, or production manager, or janitor, as the case may be, as well as that job would be done by any specialist in a larger institution.

The reader may be saying to himself that this is good theory, but how does it actually work. There is a weakness — not in the theory, but in its application. It is hard for any one man, or a limited group of men in a small business, to have the experience and the talent that are often available in a larger corporation. It is difficult for a small business to attract the kinds of people that are necessary to give it the dynamic leadership it requires and without which neither effective delegation nor adequate control is possible. To put it another way, what good is an organization structure unless there are round pegs to put in the round holes, for example — and as many pegs as are needed.

It appears, then, that an overriding responsibility of small business is to attract good people, and to dramatize the greater opportunities in smaller companies in order that the young men who graduate from the business schools will be interested occasionally in small enterprises. Actually, the smaller company is often more fun; men learn more rapidly because they are exposed to more problems under more varying conditions. Often men in larger corporations are never fully developed, sometimes because they are not fully inspired.

There is a definite need in small business for men capable of outstanding leadership — for *the* man (in the usual case where there is only one man at the top of the business) who has the intellectual capacity, the training, and the experience to understand the scientific management process; whose vision and aspirations for the future are an inspiration to his associates, however few they may be; who understands that a small business must concern itself just as much with the problems of the administrator (the planner and controller) as with those of the executive (the doer); and, finally, a person whose interest in the development of the people who work with him is such as to encourage them to seek and assume responsibility even before it is delegated.

In schools of business administration and industrial management throughout the country, young men learn to practice the *science* of management, which involves the development and maintenance of the tools required to facilitate the management process — cost accounting systems, budgets, production control programs, wage incentives, market research, and so on. None of these tools is any good unless it can be administered by men who understand not only the science but also the *art* of management — that is, the *art* of leadership.

It is in this area of leadership that we find a most unusual phenomenon of modern industrial management. The large corporation is heavy on the science — it has to be; yet the small business cannot afford this. To some extent any corporation requires men of unusual leadership potential in key spots; in a small business, however, it is almost mandatory that the head of the enterprise, if it is to grow and prosper, be accomplished in the *art* of management.

There are probably more men, proportionately, who are natural leaders in small businesses than in large corporations, though they may be a little rough around the edges. These men, often failing to understand or ostensibly even to believe in the scientific mechanisms of management, are inspired and inspiring businessmen with a high degree of commercial sense, whose dreams, combined with "blood, sweat, and tears," often make them truly great leaders. And in this kind of atmosphere — most often in companies where ownership is management — controls are less necessary as disciplinary mechanisms, though assuredly required as the basis, in factual data, for the planning responsibility.

It would seem to me that the great challenge before all who are interested in business education is to develop a balance between the science and the art of management in the thinking and action of the small businessman. He must realize how important it is to emphasize to his associates where the company is going, what its plans are for next month and for next year. This he must do while wearing his administrative hat, and he must be able to switch quickly to his executive hat to help solve an operating problem in the factory or a personnel problem for one of his employees. Or, forgetting about hats, he may have to get into overalls and help repair a machine. To find a man capable of this flexibility is, of course, difficult, but such men are necessary in small business.

Is there any real difference between the operation of a small business and the operation of a division of a large business? Is what I have been saying and what I will say equally applicable to a division management? These are questions which may be in the minds of many readers.

I believe that there is an important difference between small company and division managements. In this connection, I recall a problem that faced us in our firm recently. We were managing a small company doing about $3½ million in sales, with one of our men serving as president. Also we were organizing and developing a $15 million division for a large corporation whose sales were in excess of $200 million a year, and another of our men was serving as general manager of the division. An occasion arose in which we needed to consider whether we could move either one of the men to take the other's place.

My partner and I wondered why it was automatically evident to both of us that the man who was president of the little company could never do the job of the general manager of the division of the large corporation, and that the general manager could never do the president's job.

We analyzed the reasons why such men are not interchangeable. And we decided that the basic difference between men in these positions is not one of principles of management. It is a difference of human relations and—as much as I hate to use the word—of politics. In a large corporation a man has to move slowly and carefully, soliciting the advice of people whose advice sometimes he really does not care about, just so he can get them on the team. He cannot afford to have some prima donna ruin the program because he himself failed three months before to let the man in on the ground floor. This is not a problem in a small business.

The person who has worn many hats in a little business over the years would be likely to find it very difficult in a large corporation to wear one hat in a limited area, remote from so many of the problems which were his at one time. He would be like an old fire horse with a modern fire engine.

Conversely, the kind of man who has been a division head making $35,000 a year could not be content as president of a company where his salary would be $10,000 or $15,000; and he would not be a good president if in all his years in his previous position he had not exercised responsibility that cut across functional lines or had not practiced line management in sales, manufacturing, or general management.

So I am convinced that, though the science of management may be the same in a small business, the art is different.

Because all this is true, we often find men in successful small businesses superior to some of those supervising many times more volume or employees in large companies. I know many men who became ranking officers in larger corporations, and then, retiring at a young age, headed up their own small enterprises—happier than ever before, and in many instances enjoying a greater earning power.

An important principle to which I have not as yet referred is that of communication, just as important though less of a problem in a small company. Without good communications — up and down — there can be no adequate control, however elaborate the system of management may be.

The strength of management depends largely on the flow of ideas and suggestions from the lower levels to the top. Successful modern management depends on the consultative approach to the solution of difficult problems, on the principle that two heads are better than one. Genius in any situation is helpful; but even the best ideas can be improved on (if they are tested and tried on paper and appraised against the backdrop of other opinions). A close understanding on the part of top management of what subordinates are thinking is helpful; subordinate personnel will think more intelligently and more effectively and they will require less control if they understand more fully the objectives and the long-range plans of the company. A small company obviously should be able to maintain such communications more effectively than a large company; the atmosphere is informal and should stimulate the flow of communication.

There is always a danger, however, in practicing the principles of consultative management in the informal atmosphere of a small organization. A high level of discipline must be maintained, and this is another challenge to superior leadership. As General Clay points out in Part I, there can be no effective control without discipline. All of us have seen the small businessman who is the proud and effective head of a growing business, who has the capacity for understanding and loving his subordinates, but who also has the sense to maintain a calculated reserve. He knows how to be fair and at the same time firm in his objectives and in his insistence on adherence to objectives and to plans. In other words, he is tough; but, I repeat, he is fair.

He is the kind of executive whose leadership is respected, who can afford, therefore, to delegate with the confidence that loyal, stimulated, and interested employees will require a lesser degree of control than they would with inferior leadership.

(Note that in all this thinking I am pointing toward policies and practices requiring less detailed control attention, for the obvious reason that the small enterprise cannot afford to maintain elaborate controls that larger companies may feel are necessary.)

To quote from my own experience for a moment, the most valuable lesson I ever had was in working for my first boss, who reminded me that a degree from a university, which he never had, was of very little importance to him. It was what a man had under the belt that he cared about. Not very long after that he gave me an assignment, and I turned around and said, "Well, sir, what authority do I have?" He said, "Absolutely none. The day you need it, we don't need you."

The process of effective managerial achievement is more from the bottom up than it is from the top down. A well-managed, inspired company, with clearly defined objectives, is an organization where men go to the president not with problems for decisions but with decisions for presidential approval. But this will not happen unless there is inspired leadership—except where the subordinate is so unusual that he is not going to let an inadequate boss get the better of him.

Sometimes the proprietor of a small business is a so-called "self-made man." He is one who has come up the hard way. Often he feels that he can do a better job than anyone else. Hence, he hesitates to delegate. I have discussed the need for good men and for organization structure to assist them in delegating responsibility and authority in an orderly and sensible way, but none of this planning does any good unless the senior executive is willing to delegate. Unfortunately, the kind of man who is unwilling to delegate is seen all too frequently at the head of small businesses; in many cases he is almost incorrigible.

I should like to quote Theodore Roosevelt here:

> "The best executive is the one who has sense enough to pick good men to do what he wants done, and self-restraint enough to keep from meddling with them while they do it."

Let us consider two specific problems a small business may have:

(1) If a small company cannot afford a standard cost system, then what do they do if they need one? How can they do a scientific pricing job? How do they know what products to push in planning a merchandising campaign?

(2) Perhaps on a sales problem the small businessman would like to establish quotas and organize an incentive program for sales personnel; but he does not have the time, he does not have the detailed information to be sure that his quota figures are correct, he cannot afford to keep the records to make these data available.

In these and many other areas the small businessman has almost insurmountable problems of control. He does, in most cases, know whether he is making money or not, at least once a year. In a very small business, and in some larger ones, monthly and even quarterly figures are not available. Actually, management *should* know once a month how well it is doing. Also, if only on a spot basis, management must have product costs and sometimes even standard costs. With respect to sales quotas, the sales manager might preferably adopt only a general incentive across the board, not detailed by territories.

One thing is certain: while the sales manager may not know what sales quotas should be, the company is small enough for management to know what the salesmen are doing.

I could discuss indefinitely these details and others, but our purpose here is not to engineer systems; it is to determine a philosophy and a set of principles for developing and maintaining effective delegation and control — presumably to assure the future vigor of small business in the American economy.

While the larger corporation must have detailed controls to follow up on the activities of its many personnel, the small businessman actually does not need that depth of control, because, for one reason, his communications are better and he knows more about what is going on from intimate observation.

What specific methods are available to a small businessman as he tries to keep track of his operation and his personnel? I suppose the best, the fundamental, method, as Mr. Yntema writes in another chapter, is to watch profits. Another important method is to get out in the field and *see* what is going on. Where personal contact is possible, it is a little foolhardy to depend on controls, statistics, costs, and the like. However, cost estimation, periodic progress reports, regular planning sessions, checking on overhead and unit costs—all are methods for an executive to use as he checks on the operation and progress of his business.

The need for control is less in a company which is static than in one which is growing. However, a company which is static has little chance of ultimate success. A company must grow, and a growing company requires planning and certainly control if it is not to spread itself too thin from the points of view of management talent, working capital, and market coverage, among others. Here again, however, the need for control is considerably lessened by proper planning in advance. *Good planning anticipates the deficiencies which control confirms.* But no matter how well the planning is done, there are many unpredictables, especially in a small business, and these can be watched qualitatively at almost any interval, and quantitatively with respect to operating results preferably no less often than once a month.

In view of all this discussion, what is the future of small business in this country? On what does it depend? Is it important that there be a future for enterprises of limited size?

Answering the last question first, I believe it is not only desirable but absolutely essential to the preservation of a free competitive economy that small businesses continue to live. But they will not do so through artificial stimulation by the Federal Government. They will prosper where the following conditions are met:

(1) The products or services provided by these businesses must be essential and competitive with the best products and services provided by larger corporations.

(2) Able young men must understand that often there are greater challenges and potentialities for personal development for administrative and executive personnel in the small company, where each individual has more flexibility and opportunity to acquire experience on a varied and broad scale, and at a younger age, than is the case in the average larger company.

(3) The leadership of small businesses must stop making excuses

and face up to competition from larger corporations, giving no quarter and asking none.

(4) Small businessmen must set aside the idea that "management principles may work for large corporations, but not for me," or, that "this particular management mechanism or idea might be good for the foundry industry, but it would never work in my company."

(5) The small businessman should realize that there are certain kinds of products or services which a small company can provide more effectively than a larger corporation, and to take advantage of this fact he must research the details thoroughly and lay his plans accordingly.

(6) The head of a small company is often the founder or a member of the ownership family — often he has been taught that he should know "everything about the company," including the details of industry technology. He should, however, understand that leadership depends first on management proficiency; he can often engage personnel with technological skills in subordinate positions.

(7) The top executive, when he delegates, must have the self-restraint to let his subordinates carry out their responsibilities with a minimum of interference. In other words, he must apply controls preventively through good planning; take corrective or disciplinary action after the fact. There is often too much "second-guessing" in small organizations.

(8) The enterprise should not try to make too many products or exploit too many markets at one time. Working capital and management personnel are limited. So, one must plan their use effectively and conserve some financial and leadership strength for emergencies. Do first things first, one at a time. Do not spread talents or resources too thin.

(9) Any company must grow — so, without fail, a small company. Otherwise, good men leave and capital cannot be attracted to the enterprise.

(10) A failing of many small businesses is the unwillingness to make decisions on difficult competitive problems. The small businessman is afraid of making mistakes. Only a decisive top executive can delegate; controls are useless unless accompanied by decisive action.

In closing, let us remember that we are discussing the ways and means by which American industry can utilize to the fullest extent the talents and potentials of leadership. I believe that the free competitive system is such as to guarantee excellence of achievement. We have seen how the efficiency of people and leadership has dropped in countries where such freedom and flexibility have not been preserved.

The small business is an important part of the competitive system in the United States, and we must all continue our interest in the problems which face small business, in their development of greater strength, and in the maintenance of a higher level of control at a time when our economy is probably more competitive and the standards of performance higher than ever before in our economic history.

I have great faith in the future of small business, but I submit again that it depends largely on the development of strong men and, in some instances, on a rebirth of the spiritual characteristics which give men the courage to work in less secure situations in anticipation of greater opportunities for financial reward and community service. In small business, as nowhere else, men can feel the joy of planning, working, and controlling their destinies, with a high ceiling above them and with the room for personal development so necessary to discharge imagination and energies which are often stifled in more complicated and highly formalized institutions.

How Big Is Your Heart?

*By John S. Tomajan**

"How big is your heart?" This may strike you as a rather flippant title for a section of a chapter discussing effective delegation and control in smaller businesses. The subject is a complex one, and I have no intention of treating so serious a proposition in a frivolous fashion. At the same time, I shall make no attempt to deal with it in detail. I shall, therefore, write only in the most general terms, at the risk of oversimplification. My function, as I see it, is to provoke the reader in the hope that he will select those of my propositions which seem to him useful and develop them by his own further thought.

* Mr. Tomajan has been President of The Washburn Company since 1941. He started with the company as private secretary to the president in 1918; and before assuming his present position he served as a divisional office manager, a divisional sales manager, general sales manager, and general manager.

My observations will be based, quite naturally, on my personal experience. If I should appear to dwell unduly on my own career, it is not because I am impressed with what I have done, but rather because I know that subject better than any other and can write about it with greater authority and confidence. I am not being dogmatic here. I am simply giving you one man's opinion — an opinion molded out of some "pain and suffering."

Almost 40 years ago I joined The Washburn Company. I began as private secretary to Reginald Washburn, who was then president. My experience has carried me into the company's four plants in various parts of the United States and Canada and through different departments of the business, with the greatest part of my time spent in the sales department.

When I was private secretary, I was entirely on the receiving end of delegation and control. As I proceeded from step to step in the company, I was given varying degrees of authority to exercise delegation and control. And since becoming president I suppose that I have had the ultimate authority "to hand it out." I must confess, however, that many times during the past 13 years I have found that I can use that "absolute" authority with much less confidence and abandon than I did in my earlier experience when the authority was more limited — limited, at least, in theory.

In a smaller business or a larger one, the objective of delegation and control is made up of two distinct, yet inseparable, parts — the job to be done, and the spirit in which it is done. In other words, there is first the problem of arranging for a balanced, effective distribution of the work with consideration for the requirements of efficiency and cost. That is a *technical* problem. And, at the same time, there is the problem of doing this in a way that will call forth in each person to whom responsibility is assigned a spontaneous, enthusiastic approach to his share of the work. This is a *spiritual* challenge to the one who delegates and controls.

There are, therefore, two phases of our subject — the technical and the spiritual. The technical phase is comparatively easy to carry out; anyone can draw up an organization chart. The chart is or should be a picture of the operation of the company — of its *co*-operation—of its way of life. But a business is not run by a chart; it is run by people. For that reason it matters deeply that any executive in a position of authority concern himself with the state of mind and the attitude of every individual in his organization.

I have chosen to write about the spiritual rather than the technical aspects of our subject because I find myself interested principally in the atmosphere in which delegation and control are practiced. Top-management responsibility goes beyond the technical development of an organization. There must be concern for the development of the men who compose it. That, at least, is my opinion; and, therefore, my comments will be confined to the second area of our subject—the spiritual challenge of delegation. And so again I ask, "How big is your heart?"

As I have reflected about delegation and control in the light of my own experience, I have found that delegating executives fall into two major categories. There are those who delegate the work but who hug to their chests the essence or core of the job. They never really delegate in the full sense of the word. They delegate only with their heads. In contrast, there are those who delegate the job wholeheartedly and without reservation, the whole job with all its satisfactions, in exactly the spiritual context which makes it interesting to the head man. These people really share with their associates. They delegate with their hearts as well as their heads.

Let me give you two stories from my experience illustrating the two types of delegation. My very first experience as the "assignee" of a job was while World War I was in progress. The War Industries Board had set up War Service Committees in the various industries, whose purpose was to curtail and simplify the varieties of manufactured goods to conserve raw materials for the war effort. Mr. Washburn was chairman of our industry's committee. As his private secretary I acted as clerk of the committee, attending its meetings and keeping its records.

Each War Service Committee had been asked to submit its recommendations to the War Industries Board in a report which, if approved, would have the effect of law, defining the maximum product line the industry could produce during the national emergency.

Mr. Washburn asked me to prepare the report for our industry. He placed the whole job in my lap. His manner was such that I did not feel that I was doing "dirty work" for him. I was making the report for the industry. I was responsible for its substance and for its form. Mr. Washburn made an occasional suggestion, but always so that I felt that he was co-operating with me, not telling me what to do.

I wish that I might see that "masterpiece" again. It is buried in archives somewhere in Washington. It was a work of art, bound in dignified black morocco, with gold lettering. My heart and soul went into that job. Mr. Washburn was so delighted with it that he asked the committee for permission to include my name in the report. He was greatly disappointed when they — quite properly — refused. He was disappointed because he wanted me to have credit for what I had done. He had delegated that job with his heart as well as his head.

By way of contrast here is an experience I had later in the same year. I was handling correspondence in the sales department. As time went on I began to get ideas about promotional letters. I took one I had drafted to the head of the department for his suggestions and criticisms. He had the best of intentions, I am sure. But he took out his blue pencil and proceeded, in grim silence, to scratch out words and sentences and to insert others. Then he handed back the letter. Any resemblance between that letter and my initial effort was simply coincidental. I lost all pride of authorship in it, and to this day I remember my disappointment.

I tried again with another letter, and still another. Each time my superior's reaction was the same. From then on, rightly or wrongly, I went to that man only when I had to, never voluntarily. He was not a teacher. He was looking at the situation from a purely technical standpoint. He was delegating and controlling only with his head.

Fortunately this was an isolated experience. Throughout the years, as I have gone from one job to another, the assignment of responsibility has generally been made in the wholehearted spirit I encountered in my first experience. There have been no apparent reservations. I was asked to do the whole job even though the new assignment was in an area where I had no specific technical experience or training.

For example, I was appointed office manager of the Worcester Division in 1919. This was my first opportunity to manage. I was in charge of the inside end of sales, including sales correspondence, for our Worcester plant. With only that experience, I was sent to Chicago in 1924 to act as Western sales manager, a position in which my authority extended over the sales of three plants. A year later I was appointed general sales manager, responsible for the supervision and control of the sales of all plants and all salesmen. Certainly everyone in the organization must have known how inadequate I was technically for that position. But there was nothing either in Mr. Washburn's manner — or, for that matter, in that of anyone in the organization — to indicate anxiety. I was not made to feel that I was on trial; I had the whole job. I felt inadequate, but I felt completely responsible. The delegation had been made with the heart as well as the head.

When I became general manager and later president, I had had no technical experience for either of those assignments. However, the delegation in each instance was made in the same spirit, with the heart as well as the head, as in the preceding cases I have mentioned.

The examples I have given of delegation and control cover a wide range. The first one was taken from my earliest experience, when I was private secretary to the president; the last when I was elected president myself. The technical phase of the delegation and control was clearly different in each case, depending on the technical requirements of each assignment. But there was no difference whatever in the spirit — the atmosphere — in which the various assignments were given. I was impressed and inspired by the wholehearted manner in which I was asked in 1918 to make the report of the industry to the War Industries Board. I was impressed and inspired equally when I was asked to assume the presidency of our company. The spiritual atmosphere was the common denominator in every situation.

Perhaps a word of caution is appropriate at this point. I do not believe that, if a man just has a big heart and passes his assignments out without regard for results, everything will come out all right. Obviously, it is not quite so simple as that.

I have been trying, however, to overemphasize the fact that if a man is delegating, he must delegate with his heart, not simply give a subordinate the dirty work, saying to himself: "Well, now, I delegated the work, and the rest of the job I did myself."

I am general manager as well as president of our company. I am not good enough to be everywhere at the same time. We are a small company, within the CED definition, but I feel that we are very big when I try to visit and keep informed about our four plants. In order to help this situation and at the same time develop the management team, I distributed some of my functions as general manager.

One of the plant managers came up the sales way; he got the job of co-ordinating the sales function of our company. Another plant manager has an aptitude for new product development and engineering; he took charge of product research and development on a company-wide basis. A third plant manager has an aptitude for manufacturing procedures; he is responsible for procedures throughout our organization.

The point of this delegation was twofold: it relieved me of certain tasks and it gave the plant managers a *company* point of view. We have what James B. Conant calls "co-ordinated decentralization." Each plant is almost autonomous, yet all are tied together by this rather loose top company policy.

I could have delegated responsibility to these men in either of two ways. I could have delegated, dusted off my hands, and taken another day for golf. I chose rather to say to them, "Remember, you are doing this for me, and I want you to do it as though you were general manager. And remember, too, that I am still general manager; I don't want you to make me a poor one."

I do not believe in delegating any job to the extent that the delegator loses his own interest in it and is so preoccupied with developing the man that he forgets that he is still in charge and ultimately responsible for the execution of the job. But I do believe in delegating in a spirit which will bring out the best in the delegatee.

Even in a company where there are effective delegation and control and correspondingly good communication vertically, a problem of lateral communication may remain. Informal communication takes care of that problem to a certain extent, but there are also specific devices management may use to combat it actively.

One plan to assist in lateral communication at the top level which is used at Washburn is that of discussion meetings. Four times a year the managers of the four plants come to Worcester. These managers, the treasurer, and I have two days of meetings.

The purpose of those meetings is not to decide anything; obviously we have to run our business every day in the year, not just four times a year when we have meetings. They are meetings where we sit together and talk about matters of common interest. Over a period of time we come to know one another's minds and how they work, so that at the action level we can operate as a team.

We talk about the "list of things to be discussed" at these meetings rather than about the "agenda." We do not use "agenda" because I understand that in Latin it means things to be acted on; we do not want even to suggest that we act on anything at those meetings.

The managers are using that same pattern in their plants for their own weekly staff meetings and for the weekly meetings between superintendents and foremen. After these groups get together and talk, they go back to their own stands to do business with increased confidence and in accordance with a general company opinion and policy.

Through such meetings we establish lateral lines of communication which we hope will be freely used at all levels. This type of meeting, which forces discussion and co-operation among peers, is one way to train men to work together at their own level as well as with their superiors and subordinates.

In the past few years we, like many others in industry, have been trying diligently to make the foreman realize that he is management. We want him to be able to deal with the operators in his department in a manner that will make the operators feel that he is management, or really represents management. This system of holding meetings for discussion is proving quite effective in achieving that end.

My experience has been one long consistent lesson taught by the example of those who practiced delegation and control more than by precept. The lesson was not as clear to me in the earlier years as it is now. With the passage of time my vision has improved so that in every human relationship I instinctively recognize the presence of the two basic ingredients — the technical and the spiritual. I am convinced that only by keeping these ingredients unseparated can there be successful human co-operation.

Those readers of this book who are in the early or the middle years of their careers will not accept this conclusion without challenge. I do not expect them to. My views were not as definite 25 years ago as they are now. With what I have learned over the years my one hope and ambition is to be able to exert a positive influence, principally by example, on the spiritual climate in which delegation and control are practiced in our company.

Major Objectives

*By Warren Alpert**

My remarks are based on an experiment I undertook about two and one-half years ago. At that time I organized a management

* Mr. Alpert is a Partner in Warren Associates and Company, a management consulting and investment firm, and also is President of Warren Petroleum Corporation, Providence, Rhode Island. He was for a while with Standard Oil Company of California and left to form his own petroleum distributing company, Warren Petroleum.

consulting company with two objectives in mind. The first was to develop the kinds of skills that could service companies which depended largely on local, on-the-spot, and very often visual controls for success, and yet were in competition with much larger units more adequately financed and usually employing sizable servicing staffs but very often lacking "flexibility."

The second requirement was that the management consulting firm would have final authority and that the relationship with the companies would be a continuous one. Success demanded retaining the advantages of local owner-management type of operation, supplemented by planning provided by our management consulting group beyond the individual companies' immediate operating requirements.

Among the groups with which we have been concerned are three oil distributing companies. These companies are separated geographically, and all three were not operating at maximum efficiency when our management consulting group became associated with them. Although volume was high, profits were small.

An independent oil distributor or jobber, if he is involved in the sale of gasoline, usually represents a major oil company in an assigned territory. The distribution outlets include gasoline stations which are owned, leased, or serviced through sales contracts; commercial accounts such as truckers; and domestic fuel oil customers.

Because an oil distributor is in direct competition with the marketing departments of major oil companies which have sizable financial resources, the distributor must determine the segment of the market he can service most efficiently. He must maximize those skills and advantages that are peculiar to a local marketer in a particular marketing area, with the knowledge that in most cases he cannot possibly compete financially with those major oil companies. One of his principal advantages is being close to the problems, which gives him an opportunity to make faster decisions than his competition — decisions that are still sound and that are tailored to the immediate problem.

Warren Associates was then concerned with three major objectives with these three oil distributing companies. The first was to acquire sufficient profitable volume to reach and pass the breakeven point, in order not to run out of cash.

The second objective was to build up each company so that the people in it would consider it the most desirable place to work and would operate as efficiently as they could. If local owner-management was not developed to its greatest potential, we would lose our principal marketing advantage — namely, on-the-spot, sound decisions.

Finally, our third objective was to develop a source of future executives who had sufficient scope to succeed in other business ventures outside the oil distributing field, should the opportunity present itself and the individuals so desire. In effect, we are trying to train our management team to work themselves out of their jobs.

I became president of one of the oil marketing companies at the time the management consulting firm was organized. It was apparent then that delegating authority was essential almost immediately because of my dual responsibilities.

Company A, which I headed up, had as its principal problem that of sales. The company was located in one of the most competitive marketing areas on the Atlantic seaboard, and had had a rather unfortunate marketing history. We employed a seasoned sales manager familiar with oil distribution and also with the particular marketing area. It was his responsibility to build the sales organization. However, I soon found myself involved in making decisions not only on the over-all operations but on the day-to-day problems of sales, simply because I was there and it was too hard to resist.

I decided at that time that a great part of the problem lay within myself. As it happened, it was during that time that we established our New York offices in our management consulting work, and I moved from the local scene of action. This literally compelled on-the-spot decisions by local management.

How far could we go with this delegation of authority? That was the next question. In a small business, and particularly in one like ours at that time, with limited cash, increasing sales volume requires our making an investment in the customer's business. We own petroleum dispensing equipment and also land and/or buildings, or else we make long-term lease commitments. At the outset, therefore, I was involved in a great number of decisions concerned with financial commitments such as buy versus lease, payouts on equipment, rental terms, and so forth — most of which could be determined by setting certain yardsticks. A constant effort was directed toward reducing the number of decisions I had to make through having the measurable "facts" tell many of the answers.

A principal problem of one of the other companies was working capital. At the time I became involved with that company, the major source of information as to the health of the company was the amount of cash in the bank. It was immediately apparent that we had to know on a daily basis whether we were operating at a "cash" profit or loss. Moreover, to get volume we had to forecast our cash requirements and that involved determining what percentage of the local market we could reasonably expect to acquire and at what cost. Local management and our consulting group are constantly reviewing our forecasts and our performance in terms of that objective.

To measure performance, we provide specific controls and we delegate to the owner-managers the responsibility of making the necessary decisions by means of the operating tools he has available. In effect, we attempt to minimize the "unknown" through the factual data available, and thus have the major effort in decision-making free for areas that require judgment.

As each month passes and the companies improve their financial position, the authority of local management is increased. A measure of effectiveness is the number of times I am called on to make decisions. Another measure, of course, is the profit record of the particular company.

The danger of formal controls for a small company, so greatly dependent on speed of decisions, is that the ability to make decisions will be lost. The way to avoid this danger, it seems to me, is through the insistence of management that it review its controls constantly — and increase them, change them, or eliminate them as soon as it is apparent that there is a problem. Then management must act on the information so acquired. "What do you want to do?" is as popular an expression as we have.

Of course there are risks, both in setting up controls and in delegating authority. The cost of setting up the controls may be greater than the results achieved from them. The men to whom authority is delegated may not be sufficiently equipped to handle that authority. Unfortunate decisions may be costly enough to ruin the company—and the danger in a smaller company is greater than in a larger one, since the safety factor in funds available is usually smaller.

However, I think that management must make a decision very early in the game regarding the risks it is willing to take. And in making that decision, it must recognize that in a growth situation delegation becomes increasingly important because the skills of management are constantly being strained. Without delegation growth is impossible.

What can be done to minimize the risks in this situation? Before a problem is assigned, I try to determine the possibilities of poor judgment and the extent of the damage that can be incurred. Where errors in judgment can really hurt the business seriously, we try to "go it together."

Since our competition consists of companies of sizable financial resources and prestige, our group must develop the skills of management that will counterbalance its limited financial resources. The group has access to the pool of know-how of all the companies, and we utilize the "best man" principle. To offset the advantage of staff specialists employed by our competition, we attempt to develop in our public accounting firm, advertising agency, and legal staff the type of know-how that is peculiar to our method of thinking.

Essentially what we are shooting for and what, through delegation, we attain is the building up of a list of alternative solutions which makes it possible for us to come up with the most desirable answer to most of our major problems. As I stated before, one of our over-all objectives is to create a source of qualified management material for future businesses with which we may become associated. The act of delegation requires judgment, and judgment is the key to successful management, but in our situation we hope it also provides the opportunity for others to learn and develop good judgment.

The record of our experience with these three companies would indicate that the extent of delegation of authority and the effectiveness of controls are tied to the people in the companies themselves. While the techniques we have used in all three companies are similar, I feel that the major emphasis has been on and the major portion of our success has been due not to tailoring the people to the controls so much as to tailoring the controls to the people.

A small business in a growth situation with a constant need for cash is dependent on quick, on-the-spot decisions, often without the benefit of staff help or advice. Developing leadership is a most difficult task, but we believe that this type of operation is as fertile a soil for leadership to grow in as any we know. We have stressed pride in ownership, pride in "belonging," pride in the future of our team, and pride in building a profitable company, among many others. Through the tools of delegation and control, we have attempted to upgrade management and have stressed the need for our men to have the philosophy of "working themselves out of a job."

When I first became associated with Company C, the president of that company suffered from an ulcer. It might be said that one of the yardsticks of our success in proper delegation has been the steady improvement of the condition of that ulcer.

SHARPENING YOUR OWN ABILITY TO DELEGATE AND CONTROL

INTRODUCTION

*By Robert W. Merry**

This chapter is distinctive in focusing attention primarily on what ways or means may be used by an individual to improve the effectiveness of his own delegation and his own control. The act of delegating authority to carry out a job is easy; control to assure that the delegation is used wisely is more difficult; avoidance of responsibility for the job is impossible.

This continuance of responsibility is probably one of the major deterrents to all of us in delegating authority. What if the subordinate uses his authority unwisely? What if he makes a major blunder? Are we fulfilling our responsibility to the organization if we do not make sure such a circumstance does not arise? Can we in good conscience let matters of importance out of our hands?

The function of control is to protect against such problems. But how tight should control be? Extremely tight control will be so detailed as to obviate real delegation. Loose control leaves the way open to serious blunders by those given authority through delegation. How can we effectively control delegation without binding the person to whom the task to be done is delegated? Improving the individual's capacity to reach a desirable balance is the aim here.

For our purposes "sharpening" ability will be viewed as improving one's effectiveness in utilizing techniques of delegation and control to achieve one's objectives. If one's objective is to get a specific job done, delegation and control should help its achievement. If, on the other hand, one's purpose is to train a subordinate,

* Mr. Merry, who served as moderator for the panel session on which this chapter is based, is Professor of Business Administration, Harvard Business School.

errors of judgment, even blunders as a result of the delegation, might be expected — in order that the subordinate may learn certain lessons. Lessons learned through bitter, embarrassing personal experience are usually well learned and long retained. The problem is one of providing sufficient opportunity for mistakes to be made without allowing the mistakes to be so overwhelming that they do serious damage to some major portion of the business or to the man's confidence in his ability to survive and to develop through his own errors.

Types of Delegation

*By Cyrus H. Williams**

In the discussion of this topic there is not only a danger but also an almost irresistible temptation to be sidetracked onto related aspects of the subject. Let us understand, therefore, that we will discuss here only the know-how of the sharpening of one's own ability to delegate and control effectively. The subject, of course, cannot be intelligently explored or adjudged without taking into consideration the many phases of delegation and the various types of control which have a distinct bearing on and a definite relation to the topic. There are other chapters on effective delegation and control in specific management areas.

I think that readers will agree that *practice, practice,* and *more practice* is the best whetstone on which to sharpen one's abilities in any field of endeavor. If one is to sharpen his own abilities to delegate and control, he must first learn to do just that — practice. There are those who find it much easier to *relegate* than to delegate properly. But the more often one delegates responsibilities, the sooner he will learn to recognize the necessity of attendant con-

* Mr. Williams is Vice President of Gregg & Son, Framingham, Massachusetts, a position he has held since 1950. He was previously vice president of Worumbo Corporation and, later, president of the Diamond-K Super Market chain in New York State.

trols. Sitting up and applying these controls continually will help to sharpen his abilities in delegation.

An executive, and in particular a top executive, must have time at his disposal—even if it must be his weekends—and a mind unlittered with hundreds of petty details if he is to give the necessary hours and thought to his executive functions and to what Robert Updegraf calls "mental digestion." The only way in which this time and state of mind can be obtained is through delegation to associates (I use that word in preference to "subordinates") of all those matters which can be successfully delegated with full responsibility but with tight control. It is fundamental to an efficient organization that when responsibilities are delegated, controls are always exercised.

One of the simplest types of delegation with control is that evidenced in the instructions of one chief executive to an associate, "Get started on this and let me know on Wednesday afternoon how you are progressing." The top executive in this instance actually delegates the authority to have something done. He does not leave the subject open for discussion. He institutes action in the first two words of his instructions, namely: "get started." But he does not interfere with that delegation by telling the associate how he is to start, and he thus gives free rein to the individual to call on and demonstrate his talents. Yet control is instituted by the setting up of a date and time at which progress is to be reviewed.

For a long time, while I recognized the importance of delegation as a contributory factor in the development of an organization, I was quite confident that it was incumbent on me to explain to my associates how they were to proceed. It was with acute pain that I learned that what was the best way for me to accomplish a result was not necessarily the best way for someone else, even though we would eventually arrive at the same or about the same outcome. The discovery of the different approaches to and the various means employed in the execution of delegated tasks by one's several colleagues actually whets one's appetite for further delegation.

Andrew Carnegie was probably one of our greatest exponents of delegation. There will be some who will argue that statement, but to them I would say that his control was so outstanding that people took note of the control without perceiving the delegation. It is he who is reputed to have said, "Take away our factories but leave me my organization, and in four years I will have re-established myself." This statement could be made only by a man who had learned to have faith in effective delegation and control and whose abilities in that respect were razor-sharp.

I have already referred to the type of delegation instituted by the chief or top executive. But there is another excellent example of effective delegation. This I would refer to as a corporate radar screen.

I know of one large manufacturing organization in which the president has appointed a "methods committee" consisting of three major executives of the corporation — the controller, the merchandising manager (who is in complete charge of the sales division), and the manufacturing executive. It is the prerogative as well as the duty of these three men to inject themselves as a group into all phases and departments of the business and to make specific recommendations to the president of the corporation. At times the president will assign specific problems to them to work out. But most of their investigations have been brought about because they themselves have discovered situations calling for improvement or correction. They have come on these in their mental excursions through the organization.

The methods committee meets with the president at regularly stated intervals — the first and third Tuesday of each month, at 9:00 A.M. — and the president will permit nothing short of a disaster to interfere with or postpone these meetings. On each of these occasions, the committee reviews with the president its written report which has previously been placed in his hands, and which covers its findings and recommendations for the period just ended. This type of work is the organization radar — continually screening the corporate horizon and showing up many neglected matters in its constant surveillance.

It is vital that the process of delegation be carried out at all levels of a company, but this is one of the most difficult results for any executive to obtain. He can give a junior a job to do, but how can he be sure that junior will not try to keep all the consequent authority and responsibility to himself? How can he be sure that the best use will be made of personnel resources? An effective means of testing whether a subordinate has accepted responsibility for continuing the process of delegation downward is demonstrated in the practice of one large mercantile organization in this country:

When the president of that company has an important position to fill — top merchandising manager or assistant merchandising manager in one of the divisions — he fills it from his organization of 75 to 100 buyers. He tells the man whom he is thinking of promoting: "I want you to go to Europe to look into certain markets. Take your wife along with you. We will pay your expenses. Take three of four weeks' vacation while you're there."

When the man comes back, if his department has run as well as or better than when he was present, he gets the new job. If it does not run well, he gets a little slip that says, in effect, "It's been nice to know you. Come in and see us sometime."

I know of no better way to get people throughout an organization to delegate their authority than to remove them periodically from their jobs and consider them responsible for what takes place in their absence.

Delegation as described is vital to effective administration and utilization of resources. But too much delegation can be ruinous to a business and to its personnel. I know of one company in which the chief executive not only delegates but too often delegates the same responsibility to two or three of his major executives — none of whom knows that the other two have been given the same responsibility. They all discover it only after they have run headlong into one another. At first it was my opinion that the situation was simply a result of forgetfulness on the top executive's part. I was later to discover that, in his estimation, this was the only way to be sure that the job would be completed. I do not have to tell you that this has brought about a condition where, as a general rule, nothing is accomplished.

I have said before that the more one practices the art of delegation and control, the more proficient he becomes at it. It follows, of course, that the organization he directs will also benefit and be more likely to prosper and be perpetuated. In contrast to that, here is the story of a company which was founded some 30 years ago with a capital investment of $200,000. As of four or five years ago it had net assets of over $2 million, which of course reflected great credit on its founder and president. But unfortunately, during his many years of activity and devotion to the business he had never learned to delegate his varied responsibilities. His was what is commonly known as a one-man business. There had been no forward planning; the interdepartmental relations were extremely bad; there were no adequate controls; there was considerable jealousy between executives.

When the president suffered a serious and a lingering illness, chaos ruled. The business was ultimately saved by a top executive brought in from the outside, who was given absolute and complete authority by the family stockholders to effect a total reorganization of policies, methods, and, unfortunately, executive personnel. This sort of case, not uncommon in the annals of American business, should serve as a warning and a stimulus to the executive of today to sharpen his abilities to delegate and control effectively.

In conclusion, I will refer to a subject which is discussed in the first part of this book by Elmer L. Lindseth. That is the subject of communications and their importance in any corporation. I am going to describe an experience in my company, though in a way I am ashamed to describe it. But here it is — an example of lack of communications from the top down.

We have two forms of insurance policy covering all personnel, factory as well as office. One form is life insurance, a group policy. The other is health-and-accident, which pays for time lost immediately for an accident and for a period of two years for illness.

Recently, I had occasion to sit in at a meeting which was preliminary to union negotiations. Those attending were officers of the union as well as several shop stewards in our own organization. I was informed that one of the things that our people were going to ask for under the new contract was that the company should share the expense, or preferably should bear the total expense, of the health-and-accident policy.

There are times when any of us doubts his own recollection or knowledge. I stepped out of the meeting and called our treasurer. I asked him, "Don't we pay for all the premiums of the health-and-accident insurance? Haven't we been doing it for years?"

The answer was "Yes, sir." It was then that I finally recognized that our people did not realize that the premium was not being deducted from their pay check. They have so many deductions that they simply assumed they were paying for their health-and-accident insurance, and we, as management, had failed completely to let them know that they weren't. Of course, the facts had been on the bulletin board at various times, and other reference had been made to them, but that quite obviously was not sufficient.

I am afraid that improper communication in both directions is a common condition in industry today. Communications are essential in an operation of any size; there will have to be proper communication before the delegation that we are discussing here can be effective. A man must know what his management expects him to do; management must know what its men are doing.

An Old-Fashioned Procedure

By James M. Underwood *

It seems to me that when authors or businessmen consider a topic such as delegation and control, they inevitably look for or recommend a "new look" in business administration — a new tool for scientific management, or an entirely new approach to the problem. Finding something new is difficult in 1954. Corporations usually have efficient men in their organizations who have ideas on im-

* Mr. Underwood is President of the Vulcan Mold & Iron Company of Latrobe, Pennsylvania, a position he assumed in 1946. Previously he was an investment counselor, then assistant secretary and treasurer of Vulcan. Later he founded the Halund Company, and in 1945 became general sales manager of the Latrobe Steel Company.

provements. There are also many firms of management engineers constantly trying to improve business efficiency. People are always looking for some new gimmick, some new tool, something that we do not already have. But there is too much emphasis on finding something new. Newness of an idea does not alone assure that it will be good; an old procedure is not poor simply because it is an old procedure.

Therefore, at the risk of causing controversy, I will outline briefly a procedure our company has been following that has proved effective in reducing costs. This is a case in which the policy itself sets the pattern for delegation of authority.

Piece rates and incentive rates are considered almost an integral part of today's scientific management procedures. When some people speak of scientific management, their first thoughts are of incentive or piece rates for production work. Right at this point, the adoption or rejection of this procedure has a great deal to do with the ability to delegate authority.

I served an apprenticeship, if it can be called that, in time study and in building time standards on jobs of various descriptions. In the building-up process from properly compiled data to an incentive rate for the hourly-rated man in the shop, the bridge between time study and an incentive rate has become longer in recent years. One of managment's most serious problems is that the pace of the average worker has slowed in the past 15 or 20 years. Charles White, president of Republic Steel Corporation, in speaking to the American Iron & Steel Institute in 1951, said that in 1942 the man-hours per ton turned up for the first time in the history of the steel industry, and had moved up slightly each year since. I am not going to expound on the reasons for this, but the pace of the worker today is one of the most difficult problems of current management.

I do *not* believe that a piece-rate system offers a solution to the problem. I mentioned a theoretical bridge as having grown in length in the past 15 years. This means it is a longer and more difficult step today from compilation of time study and the time standards for a job to the selection of the proper incentive rate. For example:

Let us assume that a proper and qualified time study of a job indicates that 15 pieces per day could be processed with satisfactory and adequate delay factors. However, without piece rate, the man is producing only 10. This brings us to the bridge: to select a practical, reachable incentive rate and piece rate for the job involved. It may be decided that a 25 per cent improvement in cost is sufficient to show progress, so the rate is set on the basis of 12½ pieces, with the reasonable assumption that a 50 per cent improvement in production rate is so high that the men will not go for it and it will, therefore, be ineffective.

Following such reasoning raises this possibility: A time-study man or management engineering firm setting a piece rate in a department previously without incentive rate will have to so prejudice or proselytize judgments as literally to forget basic figures and establish the piece rate on the basis of the improvement in production that is desired. Furthermore, if this is done, management delegates too much authority to the production employee and actually may even lose control of the job.

Certainly a 25 per cent improvement in cost or production rate is worth while. A new executive coming into a company where such rates have not been used can undoubtedly make a quick improvement in costs and a quick showing attributable to his own management policies by doing just what I have described. However, the danger in this whole situation lies in the fact that the establishment of a piece rate has a tendency to stratify costs. Once a piece rate is established, changing it in any way becomes a major problem; as wage rates increase, piece rates go up accordingly. Many operating problems appear in a piece-rate program, but our primary concern with this cost stratification feature had much to do with the establishment of a policy for the slower procedure of improving costs without incentive piece rates. In 1946 we began to pay strict attention to doing the best we could on a straight day-rate basis.

Several years ago there was an article in the *Harvard Business School Bulletin* by Robert W. Merry entitled "Are Your Workers Doing Your Job?—And Getting Paid For It?"[1] The article declared simply that with an incentive rate the workers run the shop. Rates are set so that high earnings are possible without regard to

[1] Spring 1949, Section I, p. 10.

time-study pace, and changes in the rate are resisted and fought to the last ditch. In effect, once piece rates are in, management has given over control to the man on the job. Further improvement either in the procedures of the job or the pay for it are virtually impossible without a lengthy controversy with the union.

Professor Merry did not state that costs were stratified thereby, but certainly that idea was implied. His article pointed up our own procedures; it was in reality a picture of trouble that we had escaped in our policy. Moreover, it was a kind of shot in the arm, for progress may be exasperatingly slow at times, and encouragement is helpful when progress is inclined to be slow.

Our procedure is based on the premise that with or without piece rates management must fight a continual battle to improve the productivity of the workers. When day rates or hourly rates are paid without piece-rate incentive, a definite responsibility is placed on the assistant foremen, the foremen, and the superintendent to work to improve costs. This does not mean that we abandon time studies and time standards as measurement devices. On the contrary, we require more of them. Actually, more importance is placed on all phases of cost work to ferret out every possible method by which management can improve procedures or the efficiency of a job or department. But there is no powerful stratification problem. Results are slower, but if a labor-saving device, machine, or procedure is introduced in a department, full credit is promptly received for the cost savings effected. Furthermore, these accomplishments are reached peacefully without a prolonged battle at the negotiation table with the union. This is good for general plant morale; it avoids one subject for grievances.

By not stratifying our costs with incentive rates, we have retained more management authority and control over operations for the future than have companies that have used incentive rates to reduce costs. Cost and time-study work has been stepped up as a consequence of this procedure, and we have the various levels of management alerted and in position to use the information supplied to improve a job or department, because their hands are not tied by a fixed incentive rate. Finally, and of greatest importance, we have made an improvement of better than 50 per cent in our labor costs, or inversely an equivalent of 100 per cent increase in productivity per man, while working on a day-rate basis. I do not believe these results would have been obtainable under a piece-rate system.

We are not opposed to all incentives. We have several, one of which is a profit-sharing plan whose benefits are distributed once a year. Payment is not based on performance or on any specified achievement. The plan extends from the watchmen and the sweepers through to the department heads and the executives of the company. Three factors are recognized in its payments: wages or salary earned, seniority, and responsibility. The responsibility factor rewards foremen and supervisors in accordance with the amount of responsibility they assume. Perhaps one of the most effective results has been in bringing lower levels of management to think of themselves as management and to recognize their responsibilities. That is one of any company's difficult problems — to get assistant foremen and foremen to think of themselves as management and not just as the workers that they were not so long ago. They recognize their responsibilities when that recognition means more money to take home; and one of their responsibilities is cost reduction.

Results of our program are not spectacular. A quick improvement in costs is rare. But progress is steady; we are now much further ahead in this whole program than we ever would have been taking the quick cost-reduction way of a piece-rate incentive.

I am not so naive as to say that this procedure will work everywhere, in every plant, but our experience has been so successful in steady cost and production improvement that I could say: "Beware of the initial results of a piece-rate incentive program. In the long run, they may not be worth it." In the long run you can be so much further ahead on the slower method, retaining more of management's prerogatives and more of management's responsibility.

If we are to sharpen our ability to delegate and control in business, we should be candid enough to find out whether we really have the control to make the delegation mean something when it occurs. When employees are paid on hourly rates, you do not have to tell a foreman he is responsible for their production. He knows it. He has received a delegation of authority more positive than any written memorandum can convey, and, given the time and the proper information, he can and will do something to improve costs and production.

I might compare this piece-rate *versus* hourly rate controversy to the race between the tortoise and the hare. In my simile, however, the race begins in the center of an island. The hare can speed to the water's edge much faster than the tortoise. But when the tortoise gets to the shore, he goes right on into the water. His progress is in a straight line.

In my last picture, the sequence would show the hare languishing on the island where he has restricted himself, while the tortoise continues on to other brighter islands of greater productivity and lower costs.

The Crisis Technique

*By George E. Willis**

We have all heard and read many times that delegation is a two-way street. The confidence, knowledge, judgment, and experience of a superior are passed along to his subordinate by carefully developed techniques—techniques that permit some leeway but are restrictive enough to slow down any overreaching of authority or prevent a severe toe-stubbing if the subordinate should be traveling the wrong path. In the other direction, the process of delegation must be such that there is a feeling of complete freedom on the part of the subordinate to contact his superior on any problem without fear that the contact or problem will be turned into greater pressure on the subordinate.

The above precepts of delegation are repeated so often that I think we tend to lose sight of an even more important principle.

* Mr. Willis is Superintendent, Electrode Division, The Lincoln Electric Company, Cleveland. He has been with the company since 1947, having worked particularly on plant layout problems up until 1951, when he assumed his present position.

The simplest way to put it is "crises create leaders." Throughout history great leaders have been developed out of the peculiar circumstances of their eras. Moses was trained as a leader, as a Prince of Egypt, but he was not great at that point. He had latent abilities that were not developed until the plight of the Jewish people made of itself such a crisis in his life as to force their development. Without the Crimean War, Florence Nightingale would have been just another high-principled woman fluttering more or less vainly around the lamp of female emancipation. George Washington would have been simply a well-liked gentleman farmer if he had lived at any other time.

Much smaller problems are crises in the lives of individuals with less potential, but out of these crises, in the same way, comes progressive development, provided that the individual has the authority and the responsibility to work out solutions for the crises. At the turn of the century the eminent psychologist, William James, wrote in *The Energies of Men:* "as a rule men habitually use only a small part of the powers which they actually possess and which they might use under appropriate conditions."[1] The human individual lives far within his limits. He possesses powers of various sorts which he customarily fails to use.

The biggest problem in delegation in any organization is likely to be overprotection from the top to the bottom, permitting insufficient freedom of action. When I first joined The Lincoln Electric Company, I was amazed by the looseness of the organizational lines of communication and of authority.

As an example, in the plant engineering department there were informally two subdepartment heads. One was in charge of machine design, the other plant layout. They held their positions because they knew more than the rest of the engineers in these areas. When the man handling plant layout announced his resignation, he started trying to parcel out the various projects he was working on to the old-timers in the department. Time after time, they said that they could not absorb any more work; and day after day a young engineer who had been with the company only about four months

[1] New York, Moffat, Yard and Company, 1917, p. 14.

worked with the man resigning; and night after night he stayed until after midnight doing his own work.

When the man in charge of plant layout left three weeks later, the young engineer was in charge of that department since he was the only one acquainted with the over-all picture. This was delegation through crisis on an informal basis. The authority to do the job and the responsibility for the job were no less real. The delegation was much more effective than if the plant engineer had put a notice on a bulletin board, "This new man will take over and run the plant layout department." It developed in the young engineer a self-reliance no formal notice could have developed.

To create a crisis atmosphere in which the most development is obtained, a superior's instructions should be brief and general, so that the situation approaches as closely as possible the opportunity seized by the young engineer in the case described.

The one great danger in this type of delegation is that the subordinate may lose faith in himself if he fails repeatedly as a result of ignorance of the job. His superior must keep in touch with him enough so that he is certain the subordinate has the requisite knowledge to do the job assigned.

When Mr. Lincoln put me in charge of the electrode division, he followed this pattern. He merely said that I was responsible to him for the men, the machinery, and the plant, and to our customers for the product; that I should contact him on any problems where I felt his experience would be useful; and that I should keep him informed of anything out of the ordinary that took place.

Delegation in this manner may appear to be a dangerous thing. An engineer who had been with the company less than four years, with no previous industrial experience, was placed in charge of 60 per cent of the output of the company; however, again the principle of creating leaders through crisis came into play. It was not a company crisis — there were other men who could do the job. It was an individual crisis. And there were problems.

Three months after I started the job, the machine division moved out to a new plant. With it went the engineering department and all the general offices. The problem under any more formal method of delegation and limitation of authority and responsibility would have been intolerable. I was isolated in the old plant; and in trying to get on top of my new job, I did not maintain proper liaison with some of the other executives. I made unilateral decisions about things I had not even thought about three months before.

It took about three weeks for the boom to fall. A telephone call started it. Certain charges were extra because of some of my decisions. To which of my accounts did I want to charge them? There were other calls about other charges. A government regulation was violated because of one of my agreements with the people taking over our old building. How did I want to handle it?

I was not bailed out by someone else; I had to cope with the results of my mistakes myself. Mr. Lincoln never mentioned them. I am sure he was told about them, probably before I was, and I am sure he asked (because he has asked a like question of me in like circumstances), "Have you gone over this with Willis yet?" Each mistake was a crisis. I learned that most of them were avoidable; that adequate liaison with the proper people, sometimes personal, more frequently by telephone, early in the game, would remove 90 per cent of the problems.

This process of developing leaders by crisis, by complete delegation of authority and responsibility, by real belief in the latent abilities waiting in everyone to be awakened, has been proved at Lincoln. The following fact offers adequate evidence: six members of management in the past five years have left the company to join other concerns, three of them bigger than Lincoln, as their presidents. These men were trained to accept responsibility, through complete delegation. Of course, there was always a superior available to give advice when the junior felt he required it. Of course, lines of authority were drawn, although somewhat loosely. But the authority and the responsibility to do his job belonged to the individual. And the crises of his job belonged to him, whether they were inherent in the job or self-produced.

The building of men by delegating crises to them can be a basic principle in any organization. It can be practiced on every level. It is particularly appropriate at the level of the factory worker. (At this point I differ from Mr. Underwood, who seems to be suggesting that the delegation of authority must stop with the lowest level of supervision.)

All of us have come into a period of difficult selling. We in manufacturing are pretty smug about our quality and even our costs when people are begging for our goods. Last year there was a definite change in this pattern. Things we had done for years were not good enough. Costs were reviewed with searching scrutiny. At Lincoln we found that there had been, since World War II, a complete disregard of the long-standing rule that a pieceworker guarantees his output and that he must therefore clean up any scrap he makes before going home, on his own time. As we tightened down our quality, we were buried in scrap. I held meetings with representative groups from all departments. Out of these meetings came the belief that the responsibility for quality must be delegated again to the man in the shop; that our old rule must be enforced; that if this were not done, our only recourse would be to add more people with an attendant increase in cost.

Every man in our operation knows that if our costs go up, his bonus comes down. The men have had delegated to them for many years the responsibility to keep the costs in their control down. The bonus at Lincoln is not a theoretical thing. A sweeper earning $3,500 a year and $3,500 as bonus will do everything he can to keep his earnings there, or raise them.

The people throughout the plant saw the need for enforcement of our old rule and actively supported it. As a result, they have practically eliminated scrap and have materially increased quality and reduced costs. At the same time, they are entitled to refuse to run a machine if it is not in proper shape. Thus, they delegate back to management the responsibility for keeping machinery, setup, methods, and materials in excellent operating condition. This redelegation to management often affords crises, just as the initial delegation to the worker creates daily crises for him.

If the handling of a crisis is transferred from the level at which the crisis originates, delegation breaks down; and if enough handling of crises is so transferred in a company, that company cannot continue to live in a competitive situation. Where delegation is too complete, perhaps serious mistakes will be made. But in any event the handling of the resulting crises increases many-fold the value of the individual involved. In a company where delegation is overprotective and unreal, there is no development of the junior and thus very little promise for the future of that company.

Conclusion

By Robert W. Merry

A type of delegation that has not been explicitly brought out in the previous sections is that in which there is delegation of the authority to decide a particular problem or a whole area of problems, but in which also there is a responsibility to find out from each member of the organization who might have any reasonable influence on or relationship to the problem the relevant information he possesses before making any decision.

In other words, power is not delegated to make decisions unilaterally and without information — a common pitfall, as Mr. Willis has testified from his experience. Rather, with the authority goes the responsibility to find out from others in the organization what ideas they may have and what effects a possible decision will have. This is not decision by committee; it is decision by an individual, obtaining all available information first.

There is also a method of control which I think should be made explicit here — it is simply high expectation by the superior for the performance of the person to whom he has delegated a task. When a subordinate receives an assignment, or when he reports on his assignment, is it clear to him that his superior expects a thorough, competent, complete job? Merely the attitude of confident expectation, and the informal conveying of this attitude of confidence, may well provide one of the best controls a superior has over his subordinate's performance.

Let us consider for a moment the responsibilities of a superior to his subordinate under a system of delegation. Who is to be promoted? Apparently the answer would be the man who is himself delegating or capable of delegating effectively to get a job done. How do we know who is doing that, and what can be done to help a subordinate learn to do it?

One way to see whether a subordinate has delegated responsibility and authority effectively is of course the way described by Mr. Williams — get him away from his job and see if things continue to run smoothly. Another possible method — one in operation, as I understand it, in certain departments of The Cleveland Electric Illuminating Company — is to rotate various subordinates in more responsible positions and evaluate their performance there.

One of the best methods of helping a subordinate delegate is to delegate to him, making it clear that you expect him to carry the principle through in his own operation. When a subordinate reports, his superior may ask, "Whom do you have working on this problem?" After answering two or three times, "Well, I'm doing that myself," he should begin to understand what is expected.

When a man is promoted to a junior executive job and promptly takes all authority to himself insofar as he can, delegating none of it, it is effective, particularly if he is ambitious, to point out to him: "You are getting yourself so attached to this job that we are not going to be able to move you out of it; you are so invaluable right here that you are never going to be promoted. The way you can really make an impression on management is to get this job running so well that you can leave without hurting the operation."

To close on a note of caution, I would warn against the idea in delegation that the subordinate to whom authority is granted should necessarily come to the same conclusion that the superior came to when he thought about the problem. Frequently, in carrying out a job, the subordinate may keep somewhat to one side of the path that the superior would have chosen. But, with free delegation, the superior will not step in at this point to set his man right; he will let him complete the job. Then he may offer criticisms and recommendations for improvement next time — or he may find that the subordinate has chosen the better way. That is certainly one of the values and rewards of delegating responsibility.

Bei Fragen zur Produktsicherheit wenden Sie sich bitte an:
If you have any questions regarding product safety,
please contact:

Walter de Gruyter GmbH
Genthiner Straße 13
10785 Berlin
productsafety@degruyterbrill.com